SpringerBriefs in Economics

SpringerBriefs present concise summaries of cutting-edge research and practical applications across a wide spectrum of fields. Featuring compact volumes of 50 to 125 pages, the series covers a range of content from professional to academic. Typical topics might include:

- A timely report of state-of-the art analytical techniques
- A bridge between new research results, as published in journal articles, and a contextual literature review
- A snapshot of a hot or emerging topic
- An in-depth case study or clinical example
- A presentation of core concepts that students must understand in order to make independent contributions

SpringerBriefs in Economics showcase emerging theory, empirical research, and practical application in microeconomics, macroeconomics, economic policy, public finance, econometrics, regional science, and related fields, from a global author community.

Briefs are characterized by fast, global electronic dissemination, standard publishing contracts, standardized manuscript preparation and formatting guidelines, and expedited production schedules.

Yumiko Nakahara
Editor

Emerging Multinationals from Asia and Europe

In the Comparative Perspective

Editor
Yumiko Nakahara
Faculty of Economics
Kyushu Sangyo University
Fukuoka, Japan

ISSN 2191-5504　　　　　　ISSN 2191-5512　(electronic)
SpringerBriefs in Economics
ISBN 978-981-97-4041-3　　　ISBN 978-981-97-4042-0　(eBook)
https://doi.org/10.1007/978-981-97-4042-0

© The Editor(s) (if applicable) and The Author(s), under exclusive license to Springer Nature Singapore Pte Ltd. 2024

This work is subject to copyright. All rights are solely and exclusively licensed by the Publisher, whether the whole or part of the material is concerned, specifically the rights of translation, reprinting, reuse of illustrations, recitation, broadcasting, reproduction on microfilms or in any other physical way, and transmission or information storage and retrieval, electronic adaptation, computer software, or by similar or dissimilar methodology now known or hereafter developed.
The use of general descriptive names, registered names, trademarks, service marks, etc. in this publication does not imply, even in the absence of a specific statement, that such names are exempt from the relevant protective laws and regulations and therefore free for general use.
The publisher, the authors and the editors are safe to assume that the advice and information in this book are believed to be true and accurate at the date of publication. Neither the publisher nor the authors or the editors give a warranty, expressed or implied, with respect to the material contained herein or for any errors or omissions that may have been made. The publisher remains neutral with regard to jurisdictional claims in published maps and institutional affiliations.

This Springer imprint is published by the registered company Springer Nature Singapore Pte Ltd.
The registered company address is: 152 Beach Road, #21-01/04 Gateway East, Singapore 189721, Singapore

If disposing of this product, please recycle the paper.

Preface

This book is the result of the project-based collaborative research, titled "The comparative research on Slavic-Eurasian and Asian multinationals and the analysis of structural changes in the international division of labor," funded by the Slavic–Eurasian Research Center, Hokkaido University, Japan, from April 2022 to March 2023.

It is our greatest pleasure to publish an academic book as the result of our fruitful project.

We express our profound gratitude to Dr. Shinichiro Tabata, the Emeritus Professor of Hokkaido University, and the staff members of the Slavic–Eurasian Research Center, Hokkaido University, for their support throughout our research project. Additionally, we appreciate Dr. Ravi Ramamurti, Professor of Northeastern University, for being the theoretical pillar of our work. We are grateful to our colleague on this project, Dr. Agnieszka McCaleb, the Assistant Professor of the Warsaw School of Economics, for sharing her knowledge on emerging multinationals with us.

This work is also supported by JSPS KAKENHI, Fostering Joint International Research (B), Fund for the Promotion of Joint International Research, under Grant Number 22KK0023, funded by the Japanese Government. The project, titled "International joint research for constructing the theory of multinational corporations from emerging economies and for analyzing structural changes in international division of labor," is active from October 2022 to March 2027.

Fukuoka, Japan   Yumiko Nakahara

Contents

Introduction: Emerging Multinationals in the Global Economy 1
Yumiko Nakahara

**Exploring Taiwanese Multinationals: General Trends in FDI
and a Case Study of TSMC** 5
Yumiko Nakahara

**Evolution of Chinese Information and Communication Technology
Multinationals: The Case of Lenovo** 31
Takuma Kobayashi

**Internationalisation Strategies of Russian Financial Multinationals:
From Global Expansion to Global Market Exodus?** 51
Victor Gorshkov

**Conclusion: Evolution of Emerging Market Multinationals from Asia
and Europe** 71
Victor Gorshkov

Editor and Contributors

About the Editor

Yumiko Nakahara is Professor at the Faculty of Economics, Kyushu Sangyo University (Japan). She earned her Ph.D. in Economics at Kyushu University. Her main concerns are the development of Taiwanese ICT and semiconductor companies, emerging market multinationals, and the international skilled migration to and from Taiwan. Her publications include the following: Nakahara, Y. (2017) *International Labor Mobility to and from Taiwan.* Singapore: Springer, Nakahara, Y. (2020) "Emerging Multinationals in the Fluctuation of International Economies in the 21st Century"*The Journal of Comparative Economic Studies.* 15, pp. 5–7, Nakahara, Y. (2023) "Labor Shortages, Declining Birthrates and Learning to Live with Foreign Workers in Japan: Lessons from Taiwan" *Asian Profile.* 51(3) pp. 203–214.

Contributors

Victor Gorshkov Faculty of International Economic Studies, University of Niigata Prefecture, Niigata, Japan

Takuma Kobayashi Faculty of Economics, Matsuyama University, Matsuyama, Ehime, Japan

Yumiko Nakahara Faculty of Economics, Kyushu Sangyo University, Fukuoka, Japan

Introduction: Emerging Multinationals in the Global Economy

Yumiko Nakahara

Abstract Multinational enterprises from emerging markets have become integral to the global economy in the twenty-first century. Thus, in this book, we will provide a comprehensive inter-regional comparison of Asian and European multinationals from large- (China and Russia) and medium-sized (Taiwan) emerging markets. Additionally, we will analyze each multinational featured in our case study within the framework proposed by Ramamurti (2009, 2020). Following this, we will identify the limitations of the framework and suggest potential modifications.

Keywords Emerging multinationals · FDI · Taiwan · China · Russia

Multinational enterprises from emerging markets have become an essential part of the world economy in the twenty-first century.

In the industry of semiconductors, which is considered a more valuable resource than petroleum in the modern world, the "Taiwanization" phenomenon is transpiring, as Taiwanese companies have become increasingly important, especially TSMC. Additionally, as the case of Apple's successful collaboration with Hon Hai (Taiwan) on the iPhone shows, collaboration with companies in emerging countries can determine the success or failure of businesses in developed countries. Additionally, Tencent (China), which ranks 11th in the world in market capitalization, is aggressively expanding internationally with its abundant financial power, making acquisitions of companies one after another worldwide and even investing in Tesla in the United States. TCS (India) has rapidly grown into one of the world's three largest ICT service companies, with 500,000 employees in 46 countries. The largest Russian state-owned bank Sberbank has actively pursued internationalization since 2011 and significantly benefited from globalization.

Let us examine the proportion of global developing economies in the total FDI. Table 1 presents the figure and share of FDI outflows by region from 2020 to 2022. It

---

Y. Nakahara (✉)
Faculty of Economics, Kyushu Sangyo University, Fukuoka, Japan
e-mail: yumiko@mail.kyusan-u.ac.jp

© The Author(s), under exclusive license to Springer Nature Singapore Pte Ltd. 2024
Y. Nakahara (ed.), *Emerging Multinationals from Asia and Europe*,
SpringerBriefs in Economics, https://doi.org/10.1007/978-981-97-4042-0_1

Table 1 Figure and share of FDI outflows, by category, 2020–2022

Category	2020	2021	2022
Developed economics	350 billions of dollars	1,244 billions of dollars	1,031 billions of dollars
	47.81%	71.95%	69.19%
Developing economics	382 billions of dollars	485 billions of dollars	459 billions of dollars
	52.19%	28.05%	30.81%
World	732 billions of dollars	1,729 billions of dollars	1,490 billions of dollars

Source UNCTAD (2023), p. 6

indicates that the developing economies accounted for over 30% of the total global FDI in 2022. This highlights presence of developing economies in global FDI.

However, research on multinational companies in emerging countries is lagging. This is because the conventional research on multinational companies assumed that "multinational companies are companies from developed countries." Research on multinational companies in emerging countries has gradually emerged since the 2000s, such as UNCTAD (2006), the first comprehensive study. However, multinational companies in emerging countries are evolving, and their growth is significantly different from that in developed countries. For example, the emergence of "born global" companies that expand overseas immediately after being founded, a phenomenon not previously observed in developed countries, has outpaced research efforts.

Thus, in this book, we will provide a comprehensive inter-regional comparison of Asian and European multinationals from large- (China and Russia) and medium-sized (Taiwan) emerging markets, as the result of the research project by authors in the fiscal year 2022.

Utilizing novel findings of the top-notch theoretical research on the internationalization of emerging market multinational enterprises, the book presents selected empirical evidence that some emerging multinationals from the respective countries have successfully nurtured their competitive advantages by an effective synthesis of both globalization and domestic market benefits.

Additionally, we aim to adapt each multinational of our case study of each chapter to the framework of Ramamurti (2009, 2020), which classifies the stages of evolution of emerging multinationals into three stages: infant, adolescent, and mature; classifies the advantages of each emerging multinational to three advantages: country-specific advantages (CSA), government-specific advantages (GSA), firm-specific advantages (FSA); and presents the global context of firm's internationalization.

The remainder of this book is organized as follows.

In Chap. 2, we investigate the investment trends and features of Taiwanese multinationals. Subsequently, we conduct a case study of Taiwanese multinationals, specifically TSMC, and discuss TSMC's position in the global semiconductor industry concerning Taiwanization and global production network (GPN) 2.0.

Chapter 3 provides a comprehensive literature review on Chinese multinationals and multinationals from other developing countries and analyzes the international business strategy of Lenovo, the world's largest PC supplier in 2023, based on the framework of the stage evolution as multinationals developed by Ramamurti (2009, 2020).

Chapter 4 applies the modified framework of evolution as a financial multinational suggested by Ramamurti (2009, 2020) to the selective case of the largest Russian state-owned bank, Sberbank, that actively pursued internationalization and has evolved from an inefficient state-owned bank established at the launch of Russia's market transition to Russia's leading state-owned multinational bank.

Chapter 5 concludes the book, by calculating the outward FDI performance index and examining forward and backward participation of the selected emerging economies from Asia and Europe. Subsequently, it utilizes Ramamurti's framework of the stage of evolution as multinationals, examines three case studies, namely, TSMC, Lenovo, and Sberbank, and finally presents the limitations of Ramamurti's framework and outlines possible directions for its modification.

References

Ramamurti R (2009) What have we learned about emerging-market MNEs? In: Ramamurti R, Singh JV (eds) Emerging multinationals in emerging markets. Cambridge University Press. Cambridge, pp 399–426
Ramamurti R (2020) Analytical misunderstandings about emerging-market multinationals. J Comp Econ Stud 15:9–20
UNCTAD (2006) World investment report 2066. United Nations, Geneva
UNCTAD (2023) World investment report 2023. United Nations, Geneva

Yumiko Nakahara is professor at the Faculty of Economics, Kyushu Sangyo University (Japan). She earned her Ph.D. in Economics at Kyushu University. Her main concerns are the development of Taiwanese ICT and semiconductor companies, emerging market multinationals, and the international skilled migration to and from Taiwan. Her publications include the following: Nakahara, Y. (2017) *International Labor Mobility to and from Taiwan*. Singapore: Springer, Nakahara, Y. (2020) "Emerging Multinationals in the Fluctuation of International Economies in the 21st Century" *The Journal of Comparative Economic Studies*, 15. pp. 5–7, Nakahara, Y. (2023) "Labor Shortages, Declining Birthrates and Learning to Live with Foreign Workers in Japan: Lessons from Taiwan" *Asian Profile*. 51(3) pp. 203–214.

Exploring Taiwanese Multinationals: General Trends in FDI and a Case Study of TSMC

Yumiko Nakahara

Abstract This chapter examines the general investment trends and features of Taiwanese multinationals. We conduct a case study of Taiwanese multinationals, specifically Taiwan Semiconductor Manufacturing Company Limited (TSMC). Additionally, we explore TSMC's position in the global semiconductor industry concerning Taiwanization and global production network (GPN) 2.0. For Taiwanese multinationals, outward foreign direct investment (FDI) significantly surpasses inward FDI. Global semiconductor production heavily relies on Taiwanese companies, especially TSMC, and this phenomenon is termed "Taiwanization." Taiwanization refers to the dependence on Taiwanese companies as manufacturers and dependence on Taiwan as a location of semiconductor production. TSMC has several competitive advantages, including its technological capabilities, significant R&D spending, financial strength, and dedication to customers as a manufacturing service company. Given its competitive advantages, TSMC has become a core supplier, as envisioned by GPN 2.0. TSMC's investment in Japan has led to related investments in the semiconductor industry, boosting the local economy. Attempting to align TSMC with Ramamurti's (2009, 2020) framework, during its establishment, it exhibited government-specific advantages (GSA). However, it subsequently transitioned to firm-specific advantages (FSA). TSMC's current stage of evolution can be categorized as "mature." The global context surrounding TSMC includes the US–China conflict and the rising global demand for semiconductors.

Keywords Semiconductor industry · TSMC · Taiwanization · GPN 2.0 · Outward FDI

Y. Nakahara (✉)
Faculty of Economics, Kyushu Sangyo University, Fukuoka, Japan
e-mail: yumiko@mail.kyusan-u.ac.jp

© The Author(s), under exclusive license to Springer Nature Singapore Pte Ltd. 2024
Y. Nakahara (ed.), *Emerging Multinationals from Asia and Europe*,
SpringerBriefs in Economics, https://doi.org/10.1007/978-981-97-4042-0_2

1 Introduction

Taiwan is a country with a small domestic market. Thus, by connecting to the world economy through exports to and investments in foreign countries, Taiwan can achieve economic growth. Taiwanese multinationals have made their presence felt in the global economy. One of the most prominent Taiwanese multinationals is Taiwan Semiconductor Manufacturing Company Limited (TSMC), which is the largest semiconductor foundry worldwide.[1]

Semiconductors are indispensable to people nowadays. Aside from being used in information and communications technology (ICT) equipment, they are also used in automobiles, home appliances, and weapons. Additionally, semiconductors help shape international politics, the structure of the world economy, and the balance of military power (Miller 2022, p. 273). The use of semiconductors worldwide has increased significantly. In 2022, 1.1 trillion new semiconductor parts have been shipped (Yunogami 2023, p. 247). That translates to 138 parts per person when divided by the world's entire population of 8 billion people. As such, semiconductors are now considered more valuable resources than petroleum in the modern world. According to Pat Gelsinger, CEO of Intel, "God decided where the oil reserves are, we get to decide where the fabs are" (Miller 2022, p. 333). As such, the locations of fabs and semiconductor supply chains are major concerns for modern countries and companies.

According to Miller (2022, p. 297), the Taiwanization phenomenon is transpiring in the semiconductor industry, as Taiwanese companies have become increasingly important. Among the Taiwanese multinationals, TSMC has had the most significant influence. Through Taiwanization, TSMC has become not just a supplier from a latecomer country but also a "core supplier," as envisioned by the framework of global production network (GPN) 2.0. Furthermore, TSMC is in the process of expanding its manufacturing operations to other countries; thus, its direct investment seems to have a significant effect on the host economy.

In this chapter, we first examine the investment general trends and features of Taiwanese multinationals. Then, we conduct a case study of Taiwanese multinationals, particularly TSMC, and examine TSMC's position in the global semiconductor industry relative to Taiwanization and GPN 2.0.

Moreover, we aim to adapt TSMC to the framework of Ramamurti (2009, 2020), which classifies the stages of evolution of emerging multinationals into three stages: infant, adolescent, and mature; the advantages of each emerging multinational to three advantages: country-specific advantages (CSA), government-specific advantages (GSA), firm-specific advantages (FSA); and presents the global context of TSMC's internationalization.

---

[1] Foundry is the business model that specializes in semiconductor contract manufacturing.

2 Existing Studies

As Taiwanization is considered a recent phenomenon, existing studies on this topic are limited. Nevertheless, several existing studies are related to the topic of this research. Regarding the semiconductor value chain, Kleinhans and Baisakova (2020) explain that no country can be an independent actor and that many actors form an interdependent value chain in each field of the semiconductor industry. Regarding Taiwanese multinationals in the semiconductor industry, Kawakami (2020) argues that the Taiwanese semiconductor industry, which has deep ties with both the US and China regarding technology and market, has been under the influence of both the US and China amid the competition for high-tech supremacy that has surfaced since 2018. Nakahara (2020a) explains the strengths of Taiwan's semiconductor industry and the technological gap with China, which have become apparent during the US–China conflict, and argues that TSMC is more technologically advanced than Semiconductor Manufacturing International Corporation (SMIC), a foundry in China. Furthermore, Nakahara (2022) explores the unexpected power procurement by the latecomer supplier, TSMC, and compares the shift in the vertical division of labor in the semiconductor industry to a situation in which latecomer suppliers control the casting boat.

Other studies focus on the importance of the semiconductor industry in the modern world and the role of the semiconductor industry in the US–China conflict. Miller (2022) argues that semiconductors are a "strategic resource" that has surpassed petroleum in significance. He unravels the semiconductor industry's historical background and describes the concentration of semiconductor production in Taiwanese companies. Triolo and Allison (2020) reveal the presence of a limited number of actors, including TSMC, worldwide, thereby showcasing its geopolitical implications amid the US–China conflict in the advanced semiconductor industry. Kondo (2022) discusses the US–China technology decoupling and states that China's national industrialization policy for semiconductors and its manufacturing equipment is the biggest issue at the center of the US–China trade friction and technology strategies of companies.

However, no studies focus on the increasing presence of suppliers from latecomer countries (Taiwan) in the vertical division of labor in the semiconductor industry by discussing it concerning Taiwanization and the GPN 2.0 framework or by exploring the effect on the host economy. This study fills this gap after examining the general investment trends and features of Taiwanese multinationals.

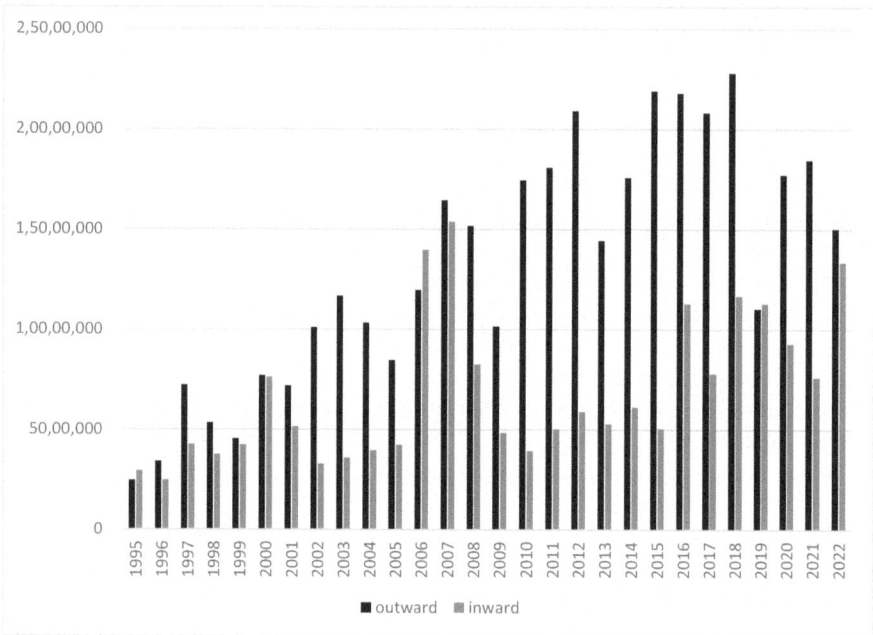

Fig. 1 Outward/inward FDI of Taiwan from 1995 to 2022 (thousands USD). *Source* Department of Investment Review, Ministry of Economic Affairs. https://www.moeaic.gov.tw/news.view?do=data&id=1758&lang=ch&type=business_ann

3 Investment Trends and Features of Taiwanese Multinationals

3.1 Outward/Inward FDI of Taiwan

Figure 1 shows the outward/inward FDI of Taiwan from 1995 to 2022. The outward FDI significantly exceeds the inward FDI.

3.2 FDI Destination of Taiwanese Multinationals

Table 1 presents the FDI destinations of Taiwanese multinationals. Taiwanese companies have demonstrated flexibility in altering their FDI destinations depending on the circumstances.

Table 1 Changes in the FDI destination of Taiwanese multinationals

Term	Main reason	Main FDI destination
1986-	Rise of the Taiwanese yuan	Thailand, Malaysia, Philippines, Indonesia, etc
1990-	Improvement in the relationship with China	China
2008-	Rising costs and improvement of labor laws in China	China, Southeast Asian countries
2018-	US–China trade tensions and the need to avoid China risk	China, Southeast Asian countries, India, etc

Source Global View January (2019), p. 66; Nakahara (2020b)

3.3 Features of Taiwanese Multinationals

Most Taiwanese multinationals belong to electronics-related industries and are considered suppliers in the global division of labor. Hon Hai, for instance, is an electronics manufacturing service (EMS) company that serves various well-known companies in the electronics industry, including Apple, Dell, and Nintendo. Hon Hai manufactures approximately 50% of all Apple products. Similarly, TSMC specializes in semiconductor contract manufacturing.

3.4 Changes in the Ratio of Outward FDI by Industry and by Region

Table 2 shows the changes in the ratio of outward FDI by industry. From 1988 to 1992, the manufacturing industry accounted for 90.24% of the outward FDI; although, that ratio dropped afterward. Conversely, the ratio in the service industry, especially the financial and insurance industry, increased.

In the manufacturing industry, the proportions of textile mills and wood and bamboo products manufacturing industries have been high from the 1980s to the early 1990s. However, toward the end of the twentieth century, the ratios of these industries have declined, as electronic parts and components manufacturing and computers, electronic, and optical products manufacturing industries have increased their shares. While the share of the service industry has increased, the share of the manufacturing industry is still nearly half even in the most recent period (2018–2022).

Table 3 presents the changes in the ratio of outward FDI amounts by region and country. In the 1980s, the US accounted for a high proportion of FDI. In 1991, FDI was allowed in China. Consequently, approximately 50% of FDI was directed toward China in the mid-1990s. In 2002, investments in high-tech products were allowed in China, subsequently increasing China's FDI ratio to approximately 60–70%. However, since the mid of 2010s, FDI has shifted to Southeast Asia to avoid rising costs in China, the risk of excessive concentration in China, and the risks

Table 2 Changes in the ratio of outward FDI amount by industry (%)

Industry	1983–1987	1988–1992	1993–1997	1998–2002	2003–2007	2008–2012	2013–2017	2018–2022
Agriculture, forestry, fishing, and animal husbandry	0.43	0.28	0.66	0.23	0.13	0.07	0.04	0.37
Mining and quarrying	**11.72**	**9.49**	**0.26**	**0.06**	**0.24**	**0.06**	**1.88**	**1.55**
Manufacturing subtotal	**87.85**	**90.24**	**65.88**	**56.29**	**67.55**	**62.38**	**48.58**	**46.76**
Food manufacturing	4.64	3.30	5.04	1.17	1.03	1.37	0.60	0.41
Beverages manufacturing	0.00	0.09	0.99	0.22	0.23	0.28	0.27	0.25
Tobacco manufacturing	0.00	0.00	0.00	0.00	0.00	0.02	0.00	0.00
Textiles mills	9.73	23.72	4.32	1.63	1.89	0.77	0.66	1.11
Wearing apparel and clothing accessories manufacturing	0.00	0.27	1.94	0.83	0.54	0.35	0.24	0.28
Leather, fur, and related products manufacturing	0.00	0.46	2.73	0.41	0.71	0.50	0.22	0.10
Wood and bamboo product manufacturing	47.37	16.52	0.82	0.17	0.10	0.10	0.07	0.11
Pulp, paper, and paper products manufacturing	0.80	0.61	1.61	0.92	1.02	0.76	1.15	0.55
Printing and reproduction of recorded media	1.99	1.03	0.29	0.10	0.19	0.06	0.05	0.03
Petroleum and coal products manufacturing	0.08	0.65	0.01	0.02	0.07	0.29	0.12	0.05
Chemical material manufacturing	3.11	5.63	3.82	2.71	3.59	4.24	3.54	2.65
Chemical products manufacturing	0.00	0.18	1.44	0.74	0.87	0.69	0.75	0.30
Medical goods manufacturing	0.00	0.01	0.44	0.89	0.59	0.68	0.90	0.51
Rubber products manufacturing	0.00	0.75	1.16	0.79	0.87	0.31	0.37	0.51
Plastic products manufacturing	6.09	25.30	3.66	2.71	3.00	2.32	1.22	1.00
Non-metallic mineral products manufacturing	7.97	9.08	4.54	1.58	2.87	3.01	3.54	0.94
Basic metal manufacturing	0.00	0.01	0.94	0.54	1.95	3.77	5.27	3.55

(continued)

Table 2 (continued)

Industry	1983–1987	1988–1992	1993–1997	1998–2002	2003–2007	2008–2012	2013–2017	2018–2022
Fabricated metal products manufacturing	6.07	0.63	5.07	3.48	4.61	2.62	1.37	2.08
Electronic parts and components manufacturing	0.00	0.12	5.68	14.51	16.82	21.24	14.79	19.74
Computers, electronic, and optical products manufacturing	0.00	0.44	6.61	11.64	12.63	9.09	7.48	5.06
Electrical equipment manufacturing	0.00	0.63	4.66	5.40	6.57	4.20	2.10	2.65
Machinery and equipment manufacturing	0.00	0.25	2.29	1.99	3.20	3.09	1.90	2.39
Motor vehicles and parts manufacturing	0.00	0.00	0.88	0.79	1.51	1.28	0.89	1.16
Other transport equipment manufacturing	0.00	0.13	3.13	1.36	0.82	0.49	0.53	0.37
Furniture manufacturing	0.00	0.06	0.94	0.59	0.19	0.13	0.05	0.08
Manufacturing not elsewhere classified	0.00	0.37	2.86	1.13	1.70	0.69	0.47	0.80
Service industries subtotal	**0.00**	**0.00**	**33.20**	**43.40**	**31.86**	**36.47**	**49.51**	**51.35**
Repair and installation of industrial machinery and equipment	0.00	0.00	0.00	0.00	0.00	0.03	0.07	0.04
Electricity and gas supply	0.00	0.00	0.16	0.26	0.28	0.10	0.10	0.57
Water supply and remediation services	0.00	0.00	0.05	0.02	0.07	0.10	0.17	0.09
Construction	0.00	0.00	0.48	0.16	0.23	0.37	0.20	0.36
Wholesale and retail trade	0.00	0.00	8.64	5.32	4.60	7.71	8.33	12.55
Transportation and storage	0.00	0.00	2.92	2.50	1.05	1.18	0.96	3.55
Accommodation and food services	0.00	0.00	0.72	0.15	0.28	0.56	0.29	0.30
Information and communication	0.00	0.00	0.71	3.89	1.43	2.35	1.17	0.81
Financial and insurance	0.00	0.00	16.89	28.72	21.35	17.79	31.81	29.51
Real estate	0.00	0.00	0.76	0.16	0.50	3.68	3.28	0.84

(continued)

Table 2 (continued)

Industry	1983–1987	1988–1992	1993–1997	1998–2002	2003–2007	2008–2012	2013–2017	2018–2022
Professional, scientific, and technical services	0.00	0.00	0.21	0.55	0.52	1.29	1.90	1.61
Support services	0.00	0.00	0.59	0.31	0.45	0.38	0.37	0.63
Public administration and defense, compulsory social security	0.00	0.00	0.00	0.01	0.05	0.02	0.00	0.00
Education	0.00	0.00	0.01	0.00	0.01	0.03	0.04	0.06
Human health and social work services	0.00	0.00	0.04	0.12	0.19	0.30	0.35	0.15
Arts, entertainment, and recreation	0.00	0.00	0.94	0.34	0.32	0.17	0.15	0.03
Other services	0.00	0.00	0.09	0.91	0.50	0.43	0.29	0.25
Other industries	**0.00**	**0.00**	**0.00**	**0.02**	**0.21**	**1.06**	**0.05**	**0.00**

Source Calculated from Department of Investment Review, Ministry of Economic Affairs. https://dir.moea.gov.tw/chinese/news_bsAn.jsp

stemming from the 2018 US–China conflict. Furthermore, investment in Europe has gradually increased in recent years.

4 Taiwanization in the Semiconductor Industry

Presently, semiconductor production heavily depends on Taiwanese companies. Miller (2022) terms this phenomenon as "Taiwanization" and posits that this phenomenon will continue. While not explicitly stated, Taiwanization refers to the dependence on Taiwanese companies, particularly TSMC, as manufacturers and the dependence on Taiwan as the location of production.

4.1 Dependence on Taiwanese Companies (Particularly TSMC) as a Manufacturer

TSMC is the main player in Taiwanization. It founded the "foundry" business model, which specializes in semiconductor contract manufacturing. It continues to be the leading foundry worldwide regarding production technology and volume. Table 4 depicts the shares of semiconductor foundries in the second quarter of 2023. TSMC accounts for 56.4% of the semiconductor foundry market. Thus far, TSMC has 532 business partners (TSMC 2023, p. 6).

In the 2010s, the top three companies in the global semiconductor industry are TSMC, Intel, and Samsung (The Nikkei September 25 2013). However, TSMC has recently become the top semiconductor manufacturer worldwide (Nikkei Business November 2 2020, p. 37). The performance of semiconductors is determined by "circuit line width." TSMC is already mass-producing 3-nm (nm) devices and is expected to advance to mass-producing 2-nm devices, solidifying its lead over its rivals.

4.2 Dependence on Taiwan as a Location for Production

Table 5 shows that Taiwan accounts for more than 90% of advanced products less than 10 nm. Globalization has led to significant progress in the division of labor in the semiconductor industry, resulting in uneven regional distribution. Less than 10 nm production is concentrated in Taiwan and South Korea, with Taiwan accounting for 92%. Additionally, TSMC accounts for 90% of advanced products less than 7 nm and manufactures all of them in Taiwan (The Nikkei August 10 2023).

Table 3 Changes in the ratio of outward FDI amount by region and country (%)

Year	1983–1987	1988–1992	1993–1997	1998–2002	2003–2007	2008–2012	2013–2017	2018–2022
Asia	**18.75**	**47.46**	**68.15**	**54.63**	**76.11**	**88.97**	**73.00**	**65.16**
China	0.00	7.43	52.67	44.25	65.02	72.96	51.14	34.69
Japan	1.42	0.23	0.65	1.89	0.55	1.88	6.07	3.96
South Korea	0.18	0.04	0.05	0.55	0.08	0.36	0.82	1.38
Hong Kong	1.00	5.39	2.88	1.37	2.29	1.68	2.00	2.88
Singapore	1.24	1.42	2.92	3.18	5.01	6.99	3.10	10.02
Indonesia	3.44	4.67	1.06	0.22	0.06	0.03	0.74	1.60
Malaysia	4.01	16.66	2.01	0.37	0.36	0.98	0.65	0.48
Philippines	1.18	4.04	1.24	0.60	0.08	0.13	1.07	0.47
Thailand	6.28	6.75	1.69	0.91	1.48	0.13	1.61	1.48
Vietnam	0.00	0.66	2.74	0.82	0.98	3.62	4.92	4.93
India	0.00	0.02	0.03	0.02	0.03	0.14	0.22	1.02
Others	0.00	0.16	0.22	0.45	0.18	0.08	0.64	2.25
North America	**73.80**	**28.42**	**8.58**	**11.05**	**5.40**	**3.56**	**2.38**	**9.96**
US	73.80	27.38	8.50	10.27	5.39	3.52	2.30	9.84
Canada	0.00	1.04	0.09	0.78	0.02	0.04	0.08	0.12
Europe	**0.51**	**3.83**	**2.40**	**1.27**	**2.24**	**0.49**	**5.36**	**6.18**
UK	0.36	0.55	1.38	0.35	0.11	0.06	2.62	0.25
France	0.00	0.21	0.01	0.03	0.01	0.00	0.02	0.04
Germany	0.08	0.57	0.10	0.17	0.07	0.06	0.19	0.50
Netherlands	0.08	0.42	0.21	0.26	1.83	0.25	1.03	2.17
Czech	0.00	0.00	0.24	0.01	0.08	0.03	0.04	0.01

(continued)

Table 3 (continued)

Year	1983–1987	1988–1992	1993–1997	1998–2002	2003–2007	2008–2012	2013–2017	2018–2022
Others Europe	0.00	2.08	0.46	0.44	0.15	0.09	1.46	3.20
Middle-South America	5.08	19.25	20.10	31.43	14.53	5.76	16.19	15.07
Oceania	0.40	0.27	0.43	1.30	1.37	1.07	2.84	3.13
Africa	1.46	0.76	0.34	0.31	0.34	0.15	0.23	0.51

Source Calculated from Department of Investment Review, Ministry of Economic Affairs. https://dir.moea.gov.tw/chinese/news_bsAn.jsp

Table 4 Share of semiconductor foundry production (Q2 2023)

Rank	Company	Country	Share (%)
1	TSMC	Taiwan	56.4
2	Samsung	South Korea	11.7
3	Global Foundries	US	6.7
4	UMC	Taiwan	6.6
5	SMIC	China	5.6
–	Others	–	13.0

Note Intel is not included in this table because it is classified as an integrated device manufacturer (IDM) and not a foundry. The IDM is presented in another section in this chapter
Source Statista (2023)

Table 5 Country share of semiconductor production by circuit line width (2019, %)

Line width	Taiwan	US	China	South Korea	Japan	Europe	Others
Over 45 nm	31	9	23	10	13	6	7
28–45 nm	47	6	19	6	5	4	13
10–22 nm	28	43	3	5	–	12	9
Less than 10 nm	92	–	–	8	–	–	–

Source Yamada (2023, p. 65). (Original: Semiconductor Industry Association 2021)

4.3 "Taiwanization" in Semiconductor Design

Table 6 shows the fabless company market share ranking. Ten years ago, Novatec and Realtek were not included in this ranking. However, they have grown rapidly (Commonwealth May 18 2022, p. 50).

That is, Taiwanization progresses even in the semiconductor design field.

5 Establishment of TSMC and Formation of Vertical Division of Labor in the Semiconductor Industry

5.1 Establishment of TSMC Supported by the Taiwanese Government

The establishment of TSMC dates back to 1987. It spuns out from the government institution.

Taiwan's ICT industry was strongly promoted by the national initiative. The Taiwanese government established the Industrial Technology Research Institute (ITRI) in 1973. The purpose of the establishment of ITRI was to conduct R&D

Table 6 Fabless company market share ranking (Q4 2022)

Rank	Company	Taiwanese CEO or president	Share (%)
1	Qualcomm	No	23.2
2	Broadcom	No	20.9
3	NVIDIA	Yes (Jensen Huang)	17.5
4	AMD	Yes (Lisa Su)	16.5
5	MediaTek	Yes	10.2
6	Marvell	No	4.3
7	Novatek	Yes	2.1
8	Realtek	Yes	2.0
9	Cirrus Logic	No	1.7
10	Will Semiconductor	No	1.6

Source Trendforce https://www.trendforce.com/presscenter/news/20230425-11656.html, Toyokeizai August 5 2023, p. 66

with the government's capital and to transfer the results of R&D to the private sector, dominated by small- and medium-sized enterprises and had challenges investing in R&D. Furthermore, companies sometimes expanded from the ITRI with the result of its R&D. TSMC was one of them. In 1987, TSMC spun out and founded a business model called a foundry, which was a contract manufacturing of semiconductors.

The Taiwanese government also made a policy of encouraging Taiwanese engineers who were working in the ICT industry in the US after studying in the US to return to Taiwan, providing benefits such as paying for their travel expenses and introducing them to employment opportunities. The purpose of this policy was to bring back cutting-edge technology and management methods from the US to Taiwan. Morris Chang, who served as Senior Vice President of Texas Instruments (TI), one of the leading semiconductor companies in the US, returned to Taiwan due to this policy. Chang devoted himself to the development of semiconductors as the director of the ITRI, and founded TSMC as a foundry business specializing in contract manufacturing (Sato 2007; Kishimoto 2017; Nakahara 2022).

Specifically, the establishment of TSMC was strongly supported by the Taiwanese government. Thus, in its establishment stage, it can be said that GSA classified by Ramamurti (2009, 2020) played a significant role in the evolution of TSMC.

5.2 Formation of Vertical Division of Labor of Semiconductors and TSMC

Before the 1980s, most semiconductor companies were vertically integrated and were considered IDMs as they designed and manufactured semiconductors within a single company. In the 1980s, Morris Chang, the founder of TSMC, established the foundry business model, forming a vertical division of labor in the semiconductor industry. In that division of labor, "fabless" is in charge of designing, and "foundry" is in charge of manufacturing. Companies in developed countries concentrate on the design process and contract the manufacturing process (outsourced manufacturing) to late-industrialized countries in Asia (Nakahara 2022). In this vertical division of labor, a lot of fabless companies have emerged from Silicon Valley. Some examples of fabless companies are Qualcomm, which is famous for designing semiconductors for smartphones, and NVIDIA, which designs graphics processing units (GPUs).[2]

As a leading manufacturer, TSMC has become prominent in the global semiconductor industry. The global semiconductor industry has become heavily dependent on one latecomer country supplier. Thus, the semiconductor industry's structure has become unique: "Suppliers from late-developed countries hold the casting boat" (Nakahara 2022).

6 Competitive Advantages of TSMC

6.1 Technological Capability

The first competitive advantage of TSMC is its technological capability. TSMC not only manufactures products; it also designs for customers. TSMC has a design support department that employs thousands of engineers with PhDs from the US and other countries. It has a dedicated team for each customer and is dedicated to customers in all processes—from design to manufacturing (The Nikkei April 14 2017; Nikkei Sangyo Shinbun June 26 2020). Consequently, TSMC has accumulated a significant number of intellectual property rights. Table 7 presents the top 10 US patent assignees, with TSMC ranking.

Meanwhile, Table 8 presents the top five Taiwan patent assignees from 2020 to 2022. TSMC ranks the highest every year.

6.2 Significant R&D Spending

The second competitive advantage of TSMC is its significant R&D spending. Figure 2 shows TSMC's R&D expenditure and the ratio of R&D expenditure to sales value.

---

[2] GPU is a semiconductor that is originally developed for image processing in games. Its ability to process multiple pieces of data concurrently has become popular among AI researchers and is considered indispensable for generative AI. NVIDIA, the developer of the GPU, is thus given attention. NVIDIA has a more than 90% share of the GPU market (The Nikkei August 29 2023). ChatGPT uses 10,000 GPUs (The Nikkei June 14 2023), designed by NVIDIA and manufactured by TSMC.

Table 7 Top 10 US patent assignees in 2022

Ranking	Company	Country	Number of patents
1	Samsung	South Korea	8,513
2	IBM	US	4,743
3	LG	South Korea	4,580
4	Toyota	Japan	3,056
5	Canon	Japan	3,046
6	TSMC	Taiwan	3,038
7	Huawei	China	3,023
8	Boe Technology	China	2,725
9	Raytheon Technologies	US	2,684
10	Qualcomm	US	2,656

Source Intellectual Property Owners Association. https://ipo.org/wp-content/uploads/2023/01/2023-Patent-300-and-IPO-Top-Patent-Owners-List-FINAL-1.pdf p. 2

TSMC emphasizes the benefits of technological development. R&D spending represents one-fifth of the total R&D spending of all Taiwanese manufacturers (Nikkei Sangyo Shimbun June 26 2020).

6.3 Financial Strength

The third competitive advantage of TSMC is its financial strength. TSMC can make huge capital investments to handle huge volumes of orders from customers worldwide (The Nikkei April 16 2021). Investments in 2023 amount to USD 36 billion (The Nikkei April 20 2023). Table 9 shows that regarding market capitalization, TSMC ranks 13th overall among all companies worldwide in 2023.

6.4 Dedication to Customers as a "Manufacturing Service Company"

The fourth competitive advantage of TSMC is its dedication to customers, as it has positioned itself as a "manufacturing service company" (TSMC 2021, p. 44). TSMC's dedication to "specializing in contract manufacturing and devoting to customers" is highly praised by customers. Thus, even though Samsung's contract fees are 10–20% lower than TSMC's fees, customers still choose TSMC (Nikkei Sangyo Shinbun June 25 2020).

Table 8 Top five Taiwan patent assignees from 2020 to 2022

Ranking	2020			2021			2022		
	Company	Country	Number of patents	Company	Country	Number of patents	Company	Country	Number of patents
1	TSMC	Taiwan	1,096	TSMC	Taiwan	1,950	TSMC	Taiwan	1,534
2	Qualcomm	US	720	Qualcomm	US	845	Applied Materials	US	847
3	Applied materials	US	615	Applied materials	US	758	Qualcomm	US	763
4	Nitto	Japan	461	Nitto	Japan	529	Samsung	South Korea	666
5	AUO	Taiwan	439	Samsung	South Korea	510	Tokyo Electron	Japan	486

Source
2020: Intellectual Property Office, Ministry of Economic Affairs (2021) Annual Report 2020, p. 8
2021: Intellectual Property Office, Ministry of Economic Affairs (2022) Annual Report 2021, p. 8
2022: Intellectual Property Office, Ministry of Economic Affairs (2023) Annual Report 2022, p. 9

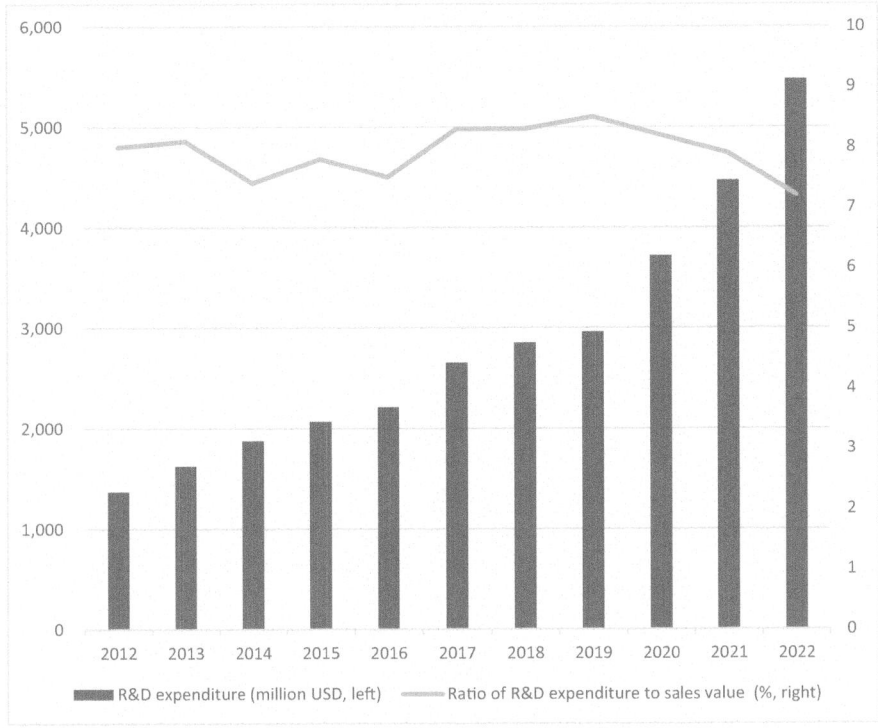

Fig. 2 TSMC's R&D expenditure and ratio of R&D expenditure to sales value.
Source TSMC (2023) Corporate Social Responsibility Report 2022 (in Chinese), p. 39

6.5 Specific Advantage, Stage of Evolution, and Global Context of TSMC

Now let us attempt to align TSMC with Ramamurti's (2009, 2020) three advantages: country-specific advantages (CSA), government-specific advantages (GSA), and firm-specific advantages (FSA). As aforementioned in this chapter, during its establishment stage, TSMC received significant support from the Taiwanese government, indicating GSA. However, upon transitioning from ITRI to an independent private entity, TSMC has thrived through its own capital and strategic initiatives, suggesting its current advantage lies in FSA.

Additionally, being the key player in Taiwanization in the modern world, TSMC's stage of evolution can be deemed "mature." The global context surrounding TSMC includes factors such as the US–China conflict and the escalating global demand for semiconductors.

Table 9 Global companies ranked by market capitalization

Rank	Company	Country
1	Apple	US
2	Microsoft Corporation	US
3	Saudi Arabian Oil Company	Saudi Arabia
4	Alphabet Inc	US
5	Amazon	US
6	NVIDIA Corporation	US
7	Berkshire Hathaway Inc	US
8	Tesla Inc	US
9	Meta Platforms	US
10	Visa Inc	US
11	Tencent Holdings Limited	China
12	LVMH Moët Hennessy	France
13	TSMC	Taiwan

Source PricewaterhouseCoopers. https://www.pwc.com/gx/en/audit-services/publications/top100/pwc-global-top-100-companies-2023.pdf

7 TSMC's Expansion of Manufacturing Operations

Despite the high manufacturing costs in the US, Germany, and Japan, TSMC is expanding its manufacturing operations to these countries. The reason for the expansion is that the governments of these countries have requested TSMC to invest in their countries so that they can secure a steady supply of semiconductors, which have become more valuable than petroleum products.

As such, TSMC has announced that it would invest in a second fab in Arizona, US, and upgrade it to a 3 nm fab. Thus, for the first time, advanced semiconductors are going to be manufactured outside Taiwan (Commonwealth December 14 2022, pp. 14–15). Additionally, two fabs have been under construction in Kumamoto, Japan, while the first European plant has been constructed in Dresden, Germany (The Nikkei August 9 2023).

However, the majority of TSMC's manufacturing operations are expected to remain in Taiwan, not only regarding manufacturing volume but also regarding product diversity. This is because advanced products are only manufactured in Taiwan, as shown in Table 10.

Table 10 TSMC's future manufacturing plan

Country	Main products	Manufacturing capacity per month	Scheduled mass production year (If not in operation)
Taiwan	3 nm: in mass production 2 nm: under construction	Over 1,100,000	– 2025
China	12–16 nm, 22–28 nm: in mass production	Approximately 80,000	–
Japan	12–16 nm, 22–28 nm: under construction	Approximately 40,000	2024
US	3 nm: under construction	Over 50,000	2026
Germany	12–16 nm, 22–28 nm: under construction	Approximately 55,000	2027

Source By author, based on The Nikkei August 9 (2023)

8 Effect of FDI on Japan and Its Economy

The investment in the TSMC Kumamoto subsidiary amounts to USD 8.6 billion (Nikkei Business February 13 2023, p. 18). This investment has a significant effect on Japan and its economy.

8.1 Effect on the Japanese Economy

TSMC's investment in Kumamoto, Japan has led to many related investments in the semiconductor industry from Taiwan and Japan. These investments have boosted the economy of Kyushu where Kumamoto is located. Specifically, TSMC's investment has resulted in an unprecedented concentration of large-scale investments and its effects are widespread across Kyushu. According to the Kyushu Economic Research Association, the economic ripple effect on the Kyushu, Yamaguchi, and Okinawa regions due to TSMC's establishment in Kumamoto is expected to reach JPY 20 trillion over 10 years (2021–2030) due to the construction of new factories. Additionally, production is expected to increase by approximately 2% per year. By prefecture, Kumamoto has the largest investment share at JPY 10.5 trillion, followed by Nagasaki at JPY 2.6 trillion and Fukuoka at JPY 2.1 trillion. If the ripple effect is converted to regional gross product, it totals approximately JPY 9 trillion over 10 years, and the regional gross product is expected to increase by approximately 2% annually.[3]

In Kumamoto, semiconductor-related staffing companies and construction companies involved in factory construction linked to the TSMC supply chain have been performing well. The mayor of Kikuyo Town, where TSMC is located, observes

---
[3] https://www.yomiuri.co.jp/local/kyushu/news/20231227-OYTNT50014/.

Table 11 TSMC's starting salary and salary of other categories in the Kumamoto Prefecture

Item	Salary (JPY)
TSMC's starting monthly salary	
Undergraduate	280,000
Master	320,000
Doctor	360,000
Starting monthly salary of business establishments with 500 or more employees in the Kumamoto Prefecture	210,000
Average monthly salary of all ages of business establishments with 30 or more employees in the Kumamoto Prefecture	288,000

Source Nikkei Business February 13 (2023), p. 21

an enthusiasm similar to that of a period of high economic growth in the 1960s–70s (Nikkei Business December 18 2023 p. 28). Additionally, Kumamoto's jobs-to-applicants ratio in November 2022 is 1.43× higher than the national average of 1.35× (Nikkei Business February 13 2023, p. 21). Hence, the investment decision of one company has boosted the host region's economy.

8.2 Effect on Salary in Japan

TSMC offers high starting salaries for 2023 graduates. Table 11 shows the starting salary offered by TSMC and the salary of other categories in the Kumamoto prefecture. The starting monthly salary offered by TSMC to an undergraduate is JPY 280,000, exceeding the starting monthly salary of business establishments with 500 or more employees in the Kumamoto Prefecture (JPY 210,000) and close to the average monthly salary offered by business establishments with 30 or more employees in the Kumamoto Prefecture (JPY 288,000). Thus, TSMC's FDI may also raise salaries in Kumamoto and eventually in Japan, where salaries have not increased in recent years.[4]

---

[4] This high salary also indicates TSMC's competitiveness in the recruitment market of Kumamoto; thus, they can hire excellent human resources.

Table 12 The concepts often used to represent cross-border cooperation between companies

Concept	Global value chain (GVC)	GPN
Description	A concept that treats the process by which goods are brought to consumers as a linear chain of added value creation that runs vertically from upstream to downstream	Like the original meaning of the network, the concept focuses on the cooperative relationship, between the entities responsible for each process
Representative study	Humphrey and Schmitz (2000)	Ernst and Kim (2002)

Source Nakahara (2006)

9 Position of TSMC in the GPN 2.0

9.1 GVC and GPN

Table 12 presents the concepts often used to represent cross-border cooperation between manufacturing companies.

Both GVC and GPN have different actors, including lead firms (brand companies) from developed countries (e.g., Apple, Dell) and suppliers from latecomer countries (e.g., Hon Hai). Until around 2000, in many cases, suppliers were assumed to be subordinates of lead firms in these frameworks.

9.2 Renewing the Concept of "Supplier" in GPN 2.0

In the 2010s, the concept of GPN 2.0, which is an updated version of GPN, was created (Coe and Yeung 2015). Figure 3 illustrates this network, in which the concept of supplier is updated. Tier 2 includes strategic partners (ODM companies); core tier 3 suppliers are the key suppliers and specialized suppliers; other tier 3 suppliers are the suppliers of cases, keyboards, batteries, motherboards, power supply, cables, and connectors; and tier 4 and below suppliers are the suppliers of plastic parts, keyboard caps, screws, capacitors, and resistors. In the semiconductor industry, TSMC is considered a core tier 3 supplier.

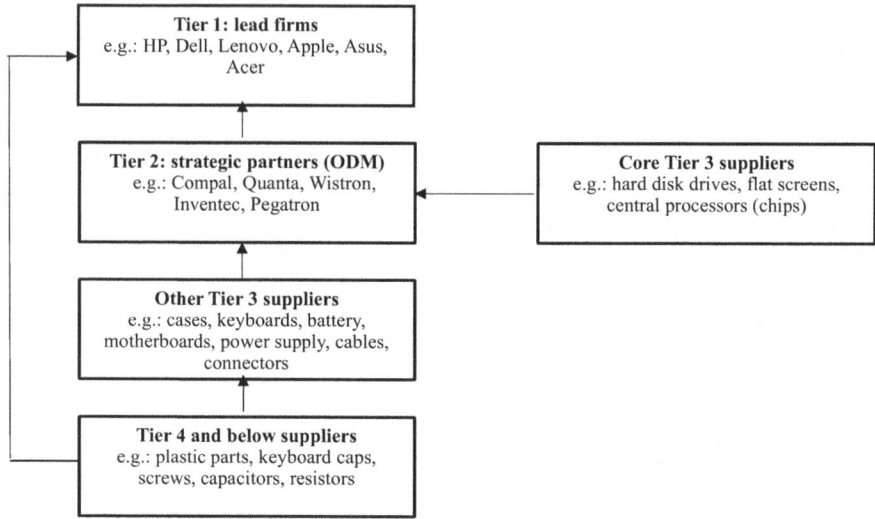

Fig. 3 Global production network for laptop PCs. *Source* Coe (2021) Fig. 1.2 (p. 5). *Note* I only extracted the lead firms, strategic partners, and suppliers from the original figure and added some supplementary explanations. Additionally, the arrows represent the dashed lines in the original figure

10 Conclusion

This chapter first investigates the investment trends and features of Taiwanese multinationals; then, we focus on TSMC. We examine TSMC's position in the global semiconductor industry through Taiwanization and GPN 2.0.

Our findings show that outward FDI is significantly larger than inward FDI. Regarding the ratio of FDI by industry, the manufacturing industry accounted for over 90% in 1990 although the percentage dropped afterward. Conversely, the ratio of the service industry, especially that of the financial and insurance industry, has increased. While the ratio of the manufacturing industry has decreased, it is still nearly half of the total FDI in the most recent period (2018–2022). In the 1980s, FDI to the US accounts for a high proportion. However, in the mid-1990s, China's share has slowly increased. Since the mid of 2010s, FDI has been shifted to Southeast Asia to avoid rising costs in China, the risk of excessive concentration in China, and the risks associated with the 2018 US–China conflict.

Presently, semiconductors have become increasingly significant. The production of semiconductors relies heavily on Taiwanese companies, especially TSMC. This heavy dependence is called Taiwanization. In Taiwanization, TSMC is not considered a subordinate of lead firms from developed countries.

In Miller's book, "Taiwanization" refers to the concentration of semiconductor production. In recent years, Taiwanese companies have also demonstrated a large presence in semiconductor design (fabless) as well as a high share in the fabless market.

TSMC was spun out from the government institution by the returnee who was invited by the Taiwanese government which expected returnees to bring back cutting-edge technology and management methods from the US to Taiwan. Thus the establishment of TSMC was strongly supported by the Taiwanese government.

TSMC has several competitive advantages that make it a leading player in the industry. First is its technological capability, as the company is not only involved in the production but also in the design process. Second is its significant R&D spending, which amounts to one-fifth of the total R&D spending of all manufacturers in Taiwan. Third is its financial strength, as it can attract significant investments to handle orders from customers worldwide. Fourth is its dedication to customers as a "manufacturing service company." Thus, TSMC has become a core supplier, as envisioned by GPN 2.0, taking a different position from former latecomer suppliers.

Furthermore, TSMC has been expanding its manufacturing bases to the US, Germany, and Japan upon the request of the governments of these countries. TSMC's FDI in Kumamoto, Japan has led to many related investments in the semiconductor industry from Taiwan and Japan. These investments have invigorated the economy of the Kyushu region where Kumamoto is located.

If we attempt to adapt TSMC to Ramamurti's (2009, 2020) three advantages, during its establishment stage, it received strong support from the Taiwanese government, indicating GSA. However, subsequently, it successfully evolved through its own capital and strategic initiatives. Thus, TSMC's current advantage can be categorized as FSA. Additionally, as a key player in Taiwanization on a global scale, TSMC's stage of evolution can be considered "mature." In the global context surrounding TSMC, factors such as the US–China conflict and the increasing global demand for semiconductors are noteworthy.

References

Coe NM, Yeung HW-C (2015) Global production networks: theorizing economic development in an interconnected world. Oxford University Press, Oxford
Coe NM (2021) Advanced introduction to global production networks. Edward Elgar, Cheltenham
Ernst D, Kim L (2002) Global production networks, knowledge diffusion, and local capability formation. Res Policy 31(8–9):1417–1429
Humphrey J, Schmitz H (2000) Governance and upgrading: linking industrial cluster and global value chain research. IDS Working Paper 120, Institute of Development Studies, University of Sussex
Intellectual Property Office, Ministry of Economic Affairs (2021) Annual report 2020 (in Chinese)
Intellectual Property Office, Ministry of Economic Affairs (2022) Annual report 2021 (in Chinese)
Intellectual Property Office, Ministry of Economic Affairs (2023) Annual report 2022 (in Chinese)
Kawakami M (2020) US-China high-tech competition and the Taiwanese IC industry: under the influence of two magnetic fields. In: Kawashima S, Mori S (ed) U.S.-China relations and the world order after COVID-19. The University of Tokyo Press, Tokyo, pp 131–139 (in Japanese)

Kishimoto C (2017) The competitive strategy of Taiwanese semiconductor enterprises: the evolution of strategy and capability building. Nippon Hyoron Sha Co., Ltd, Tokyo (in Japanese)

Kondo S (2022) Technical position of China's high-tech industry: trade friction between US and China's high-tech industry and technology decoupling in the semiconductor industry. In: Nakamoto S, Matsumura H (ed) The political economy of the US-China economic friction. Koyo Shobo, Kyoto, pp 117–139 (in Japanese)

Kleinhans J, Baisakova N (2020) The global semiconductor value chain: a technology primer for policy makers. Think Tank at the Intersection of Technology and Society

Miller C (2022) Chip war: the fight for the world's most critical technology. Simon & Schuster Ltd., New York

Nakahara Y (2006) The development of Taiwanese PC industry and the global production network: from the learning point of view. Doctoral dissertation of Graduate School of Economics. Kyushu University (in Japanese)

Nakahara Y (2020a) Strengths of Taiwan's semiconductor industry and technological gap with China: focusing on TSMC and SMIC. East Asia 640:18–25 (in Japanese)

Nakahara Y (2020b) Taiwanese company in the 21st century: in the change of international economy. In: Asamoto T, Nakahara Y (eds) Researches of Taiwanese companies. Kyushu University Press, Fukuoka, pp 1–35 (in Japanese)

Nakahara Y (2022) The change of vertical division of labor of the semiconductor industry. J Asian Manag Stud 28:39–51 (in Japanese)

Ramamurti R (2009) What have we learned about emerging-market MNEs? In: Ramamurti R, Singh JV (eds) Emerging multinationals in emerging markets. Cambridge University Press, Cambridge, pp 399-426

Ramamurti R (2020) Analytical misunderstandings about emerging-market multinationals. J Comp Econ Stud 15:9–20

Sato Y (2007) Formation and development of Taiwan's high-tech industries. Iwanami Shoten, Tokyo (in Japanese)

Statista (2023) Semiconductor foundries revenue share worldwide from 2019 to 2023, by quarter. https://www.statista.com/statistics/867223/worldwide-semiconductor-foundries-by-market-share/

Triolo P, Allison K (2020) The geopolitics of semiconductors. https://www.eurasiagroup.net/

TSMC (2021) Corporate social responsibility report 2020 (in Chinese)

TSMC (2023) Corporate social responsibility report 2022 (in Chinese)

Yamada S (2023) Why the world depends on this company? TSMC's global strategy and the challenge of geopolitical risk. Toyokeizai 7129:64–65 (in Japanese)

Yunogami T (2023) Semiconductor emergency. Bungeishunju. Tokyo (in Japanese)

Periodicals

Commonwealth: 748 May 18 2022. 763 December 14 2022
Global View: 391 January 2019
Nikkei Business: 2064 November 2 2020. 2178 February 13 2023. 2221 December 18 2023
Nikkei Sangyo Shinbun: June 25 2020. June 26 2020
The Nikkei: September 25 2013. April 14 2017. April 16 2021. April 20 2023. June 14 2023. August 9 2023. August 10 2023. August 29 2023
Toyokeizai: 7129 August 5 2023

Yumiko Nakahara is professor at the Faculty of Economics, Kyushu Sangyo University (Japan). She earned her Ph.D. in Economics at Kyushu University. Her main concerns are the development of Taiwanese ICT and semiconductor companies, emerging market multinationals, and the international skilled migration to and from Taiwan. Her publications include the following: Nakahara, Y. (2017) *International Labor Mobility to and from Taiwan*. Singapore: Springer, Nakahara, Y. (2020) "Emerging Multinationals in the Fluctuation of International Economies in the 21st Century" *The Journal of Comparative Economic Studies*. 15, pp. 5–7, Nakahara, Y. (2023) "Labor Shortages, Declining Birthrates and Learning to Live with Foreign Workers in Japan: Lessons from Taiwan" *Asian Profile*. 51(3) pp. 203–214.

Evolution of Chinese Information and Communication Technology Multinationals: The Case of Lenovo

Takuma Kobayashi

Abstract In the 2000s, China's outward Foreign Direct Investment increased rapidly. A total of 135 Chinese enterprises were ranked in the Fortune Global 500 by 2023. However, many of them lack firm-specific advantages (FSAs) and are more dependent on country-specific advantages (CSAs); most of their sales are generated in China. This chapter analyses the extent to which Lenovo, a Chinese Information and Communication Technology enterprise, has evolved as a multinational enterprise (MNE) in terms of (i) FSAs, (ii) CSAs, (iii) export/overseas production ratio, and (iv) geographical footprints. Lenovo has reached a mature stage regarding FSAs, as it has enhanced its Research and Development capabilities and built a world-renowned brand. In terms of geographical footprints, Lenovo has reached a mature stage, as it has subsidiaries in many countries worldwide and significant sales overseas. However, Lenovo is still in its infancy regarding CSAs, as it was originally a state institution with strong government relations. In addition, Lenovo is still in its infancy with regard to its export/overseas production ratio, as a large number of personal computers are produced in Asia. Therefore, Lenovo is currently in the adolescent stage as an MNE.

Keywords Evolution of Chinese multinationals · Firm-specific advantages · Country-specific advantages · Export/overseas production ratio · Geographical footprints

1 Introduction

China implemented its reform and open-door policy in 1978 by introducing foreign investments. At that time, it was limited to a few regions, such as special economic zones. Foreign direct investment (FDI) in China in the 1980s amounted to only USD 1–3 billion per year. However, FDI in China increased rapidly after Deng Xiaoping's 1992 Southern Tours Speech, reaching more than 100 billion USD in 2008. In the

T. Kobayashi (✉)
Faculty of Economics, Matsuyama University, Matsuyama, Ehime, Japan
e-mail: tkobayas@g.matsuyama-u.ac.jp

© The Author(s), under exclusive license to Springer Nature Singapore Pte Ltd. 2024
Y. Nakahara (ed.), *Emerging Multinationals from Asia and Europe*,
SpringerBriefs in Economics, https://doi.org/10.1007/978-981-97-4042-0_3

2000s, China's outward FDI began to increase faster than its inward FDI, and both were almost at the same level. In 2022, China ranked second in the world with a flow of USD 163.12 billion, and third in the world with a stock of USD 2,745.81 billion (Ministry of Commerce of the People's Republic of China et al. 2023).

An increasing number of Chinese enterprises are generating high global revenues. In 2012, 73 Chinese enterprises (including Hong Kong) were ranked in the Fortune Global 500, by the US economic magazine Fortune, compared with the 68 Japanese enterprises. However, according to Rugman and Nguen (2014), most of these were state-owned enterprises and majority of their sales were generated within China. They were predominantly from industries such as banking, insurance, natural resources, utilities, telecommunications, land and property development, engineering, and construction. They were based on country-specific advantages (CSAs), such as low labour costs, economies of scale, subsidised capital, and privileged access to government links. If multinational enterprises (MNEs) are defined as enterprises operating in three countries other than their headquarters, generating more than 10% of their turnover abroad, and producing through FDI, then in 2012, only five enterprises in China could be called MNEs. These included the Noble Group, Hutchison Whampoa (two Hong Kong enterprises), Huawei Investment and Holding, Lenovo Group, and China Ocean Shipping (three Mainland China enterprises). This chapter focusses on Lenovo among these enterprises and analyses how it has evolved as an MNE with firm-specific advantages using the evolutionary theory of MNE proposed by Ramamurti (2009, 2020).

The structure of this chapter is as follows: in Sect. 2 we show the evolution of China's outward FDI; in Sect. 3 we briefly introduce the literature review on MNEs from developed countries and provide a comprehensive literature review on Chinese MNEs and MNEs from other developing countries; in Sect. 4 we describe the analytical framework of the stage evolution as an MNE; in Sect. 5 we analyse the extent to which Lenovo has evolved as an MNE based on the framework described in Sect. 4; finally, we summarise the contents of this chapter and discuss future research question.

2 China's Outward FDI

Until the beginning of the reform and open-door policy, Chinese enterprises only developed their overseas activities in conjunction with government foreign economic development assistance projects. In 1979, the State Council approved the establishment of domestic enterprises abroad (Jiang 2020). However, as China suffered trade and foreign currency shortages caused by weak export competitiveness, it designed foreign investment and currency management policies to ensure that it received more foreign currency than it paid out. Until the early 1990s, foreign enterprises were required to receive more foreign currency than what they paid at the individual enterprise level. Reforms to the foreign exchange management system in 1994 eliminated many of these restrictions; however, institutions restricting foreign currency payments remained (Marukawa 2008).

When China began implementing its 'going global' strategy in 1999 and joined the World Trade Organization in 2001, outward FDI by Chinese enterprises was greatly promoted. In 2004, the number of documents previously required for enterprises wishing to make outward FDIs to obtain approval from the Ministry of Commerce, such as proof of import and export values and a feasibility study of the investment project, was reduced. In addition, the screening procedure for outward FDI projects was simplified. Furthermore, in terms of taxation, dividend income from overseas subsidiaries was exempt from corporate income tax in China for 5 years after the local subsidiary turned profitable, and export tariffs on equipment and machinery for investment were exempt. On the financial side, the National Development and Reform Commission and the Export–Import Bank of China initiated financial support policies for overseas investments, granting loans at preferential interest rates for overseas resource development, factory and infrastructure construction, research and development (R&D), and acquisitions (Marukawa 2008).

As a result of the deregulation and introduction of the preferential policies mentioned above, Chinese outward FDI has increased significantly since 2004.

By the end of 2022, 29,000 Chinese domestic investors had established 46.6 thousand FDI enterprises[1] overseas in 190 countries and regions worldwide. In 2022, outward FDI stock reached 2754.81 billion dollars, which is 30.4 times that in 2006 (Fig. 1). It accounts for 6.9% of the global total, ranking third[2] after the US and the Netherlands, among all countries and regions. This was only 28.4% of that in the US (Fig. 2).

3 Logic Behind Enterprises' Overseas Expansion

This section first introduces the traditional theory regarding the logic of the motives of enterprises from developed countries to expand overseas and then explains the motives of MNEs from developing countries, including Chinese MNEs, to expand overseas.

3.1 Mainstream Traditional MNE Theories

Hymer (1976) explains that MNEs seek to expand their operations internationally through FDI because they expect to make more profits than local enterprises, owing to

---

[1] FDI enterprises refer to foreign enterprises that are directly owned or have 10% (or above) voting rights and equivalents controlled by domestic investors.

[2] China's outward FDI stock ranked second in the world in 2017 and third from 2018 to 2022.

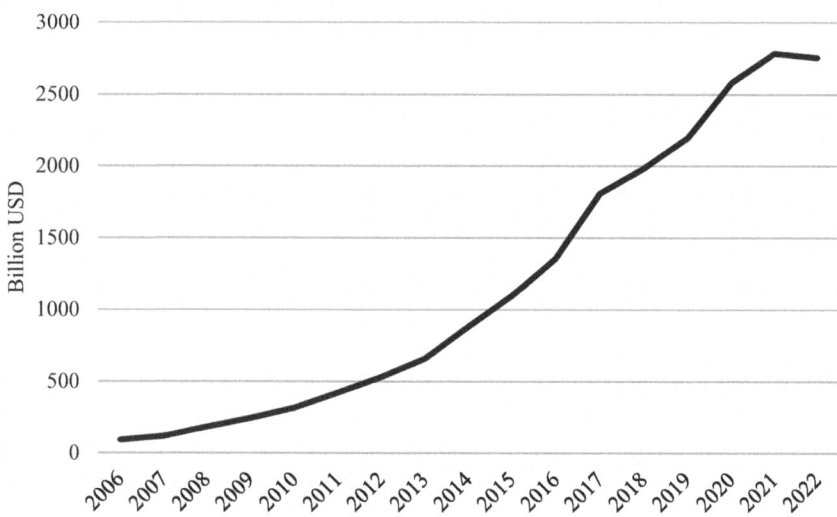

Fig. 1 China's outward FDI stock. *Source* Ministry of Commerce of the People's Republic of China et al. (2023)

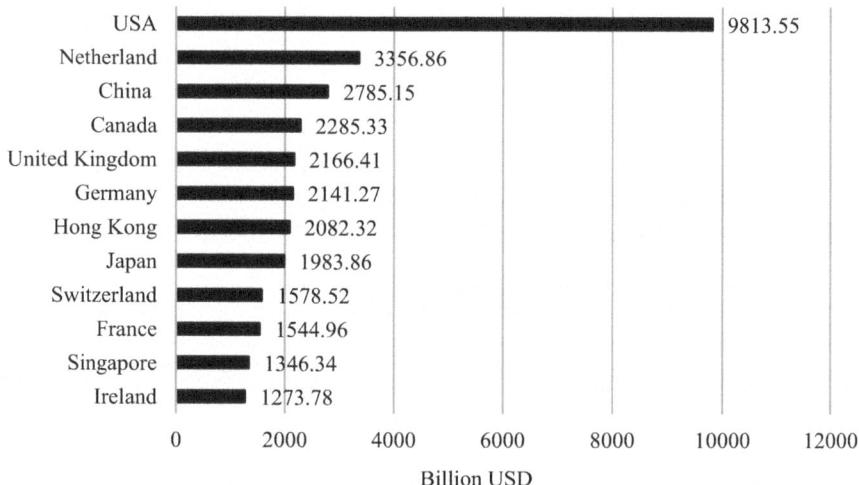

Fig. 2 Outward FDI stock of China and other major countries and regions. *Source* Ministry of Commerce of the People's Republic of China et al. (2023)

their advantages in technology (e.g. manufacturing technology, product development capabilities, and business management), knowledge of human resource development and distribution, and product differentiation capabilities.

According to Vernon (1966), new products follow the lifecycle of introduction, growth, maturity, and decline. When a product reaches maturity, competition over price increases, making use of low-cost labour abroad more attractive to enterprises. However, low labour costs alone are not a decisive factor for FDI in overseas production, as enterprises must take different risks in overseas production than in domestic production. Furthermore, when products reach the standardisation stage, production technology becomes obsolete, and the production of imitations and similar products abroad, which threatens their status as innovative enterprises, is a trigger for FDIs.

A group from the University of Reading in the UK argue that when imperfections exist in the market, it is more advantageous for MNEs to absorb and directly control their overseas activities within the enterprise, rather than leaving them to market mechanisms (Buckley and Casson 1991). The internalisation theory argues that enterprises embark on their own production and sales through direct investment to avoid sharing information and know-how on product development, production, and sales with other enterprises, and to use it exclusively (Yuan 2014, p. 57).

J. H. Dunning believes that three advantages—ownership, location, and internalisation—are important for an enterprise's decision to expand abroad. First, ownership-specific advantage is the possession of capabilities, such as technology, management-related competencies, or access to various management resources that are specific to an enterprise. Second, location-specific advantages refer to the ability to reduce various costs and risks by producing locally rather than exporting from the home country, and easier access to raw materials and other resources and distribution channels by being in the host country. Third, internalisation advantage refers to the case in which suitable partners cannot be found locally, when insufficient attention is given to the enterprise's brand image and strategy, when information relating to the enterprise's products are leaked, and when the costs of entering and maintaining such partnerships are considered, the enterprise decides that establishing a subsidiary is more appropriate than having an external enterprise as a partner (Dunning 1979).

The traditional theory described above defines the patterns of MNEs' overseas expansions from developed countries. The MNEs from developed countries have the following characteristics. First, there are very few or no international MNEs in the sector in the early years of an enterprise's multinational operations. Second, an enterprise's core technology is self-invented and developed (Kang 2013, p. 19).

3.2 Theories of MNEs from Developing Countries

Since the 1990s, enterprises in developing countries have been engaging in outward FDIs, despite their lack of competitiveness. This has led to an increase in research on the motives of MNEs from developing countries and Chinese MNEs to go abroad. The characteristics of MNEs from developing countries are, first, that there are already several MNEs in the international market of the sector when the relevant MNEs start internationalisation, and second, the core technology of the relevant MNEs is mainly introduced from abroad (Kang 2013, p. 19).

The United Nations Conference on Trade and Development (2006) identified the following motivations for MNEs from developing countries: market-seeking in low- and middle-income countries, efficiency-seeking to enter countries with low labour costs to reduce production costs, resource-seeking to secure natural resources, created asset-seeking to acquire superior management resources of foreign enterprises and others to acquire national strategic resources, and acquiring knowledge as a latecomer's benefit as a nation. The most noteworthy of these is asset-seeking. In this type of FDI, it is not necessarily assumed that the enterprise has firm-specific advantages (FSAs) in advance but rather that it acquires a competitive advantage after the investment has been made.

Marukawa (2008) categorised Chinese enterprises' outward FDIs into five categories: (1) developing backward markets (competitive advantage type according to Hymer (1976), (2) acquiring strategic assets, (3) raising overseas funds,[3] (4) improving efficiency, and (5) vertical integration of upstream sectors across borders.[4]

Yuan (2014) proposed a hypothesis for MNEs from developing countries. They have emerged since the 1990s and expanded in developing countries; unlike MNEs from developed countries, they have direct investment and conduct local production and management activities in one or more countries or regions other than their home country. Yuan (2014) classified the competitive advantages possessed by MNCs into regular and irregular. Regular competitive advantage is proposed by Hymer (1976) and Dunning (1979). Irregular competitive advantage includes social capital elements, such as social trust, norms, and networks, and innovative combinations, such as the ability to discover and judge markets and goods and the ability to imitate product technology. Chinese enterprises have few regular competitive advantages; therefore, they cover their inferiority by introducing various locally accepted competitive instruments (such as informal relationships, contacts, and connections) (Yuan 2014, p. 108).

Liu (2014) states that Chinese MNEs have 'idiosyncrasies', the so-called 'reverse phenomenon', when compared to MNEs from developed countries with regard to their overseas expansion. First, enterprises acquire FSAs after overseas expansion, rather than before expanding overseas. Lenovo and TCL acquired advantages that they lacked at the time of their overseas expansion by acquiring superior resources (technology, brand, R&D team, etc.) from foreign enterprises. Second, owing to a lack of trust in domestic consumers, rather than penetrating the domestic market and enhancing its position before expanding overseas, Haier entered overseas from the initial stage and refined itself and its products in mature developed markets.

---

[3] As China's capital markets are imperfect, they raise funds by listing on overseas stock markets, such as NASDAQ, and invest these funds in China (Marukawa 2008).

[4] Marukawa (2008) sees the motivation for enterprises in the natural resource extraction industry to expand outward not as a national policy to secure resources, but because they can reduce transaction costs by acquiring oil fields and mines abroad.

Haier dared to focus on developing developed markets in Europe and the US, where specifications and standards are more demanding; in the early stages of internationalisation, and by gaining recognition and trust there, it was later able to enter developing markets such as Southeast Asia and Latin America, where it was relatively less difficult to make inroads. Third, rather than targeting the Top of the Pyramid (TOP) market or upper echelons of the Middle of the Pyramid (MOP) market, such as MNEs from developed countries, MNEs from developing countries targeted the Base of the Pyramid (BOP) before entering the upper echelons of the MOP or TOP markets. For example, Huawei started its success domestically, in rural areas, and then expanded to urban areas in earnest, while overseas expansion started in countries and regions with low income levels. After accumulating further business experience, technology, and capital, it entered developed countries with high income levels and high technology levels, such as Europe, the US, and Japan.

Nakagawa (2017) proposed the theory of middle-income country MNEs, which states that China, as a middle-income country, will expand with competitive advantages to countries at the same or less developed level, while moving to acquire strategic assets in countries that are more developed than China.

Yuan (2023) summarises the characteristics of Chinese MNEs as follows. First, they have a strong orientation towards developing regions in their choice of investment locations. Second, publicly owned and private enterprises coexist as investment entities (see Fig. 3). Third, there is a strong orientation towards strategic asset acquisition. Fourth, there is strong M&A orientation regarding investment methods. Fifth, there are many irregular competitive factors. Sixth, an advantage lacking at the time of expanding abroad is acquired through foreign enterprises' acquisition of superior resources. Alternatively, even when expanding overseas independently, an enterprise acquires and demonstrates its advantage by learning from market competition in the host country. Seventh, there is strong localisation from the beginning of the expansion. Eighth, the enterprise enters the MOP/TOP market after establishing an overseas presence by targeting the lower tier of the volume zone market, the BOP market, as part of its overseas local market strategy.

4 Framework of Stage Evolution as an MNE

Section 3 provides a review of the MNE theory, noting that in recent years, there has been an increase in the analysis of MNEs from developing countries and of MNEs from China, where outward FDIs have been increasing rapidly.

Ramamurti (2020), a prominent researcher in international business, stated that nationality is of little analytical value in understanding an enterprise's internationalisation. It is important to recognise that every country is unique, but this does not mean that we need a unique theory of internationalisation for each country. The goal of theory building is to find variables that are analytically useful across different

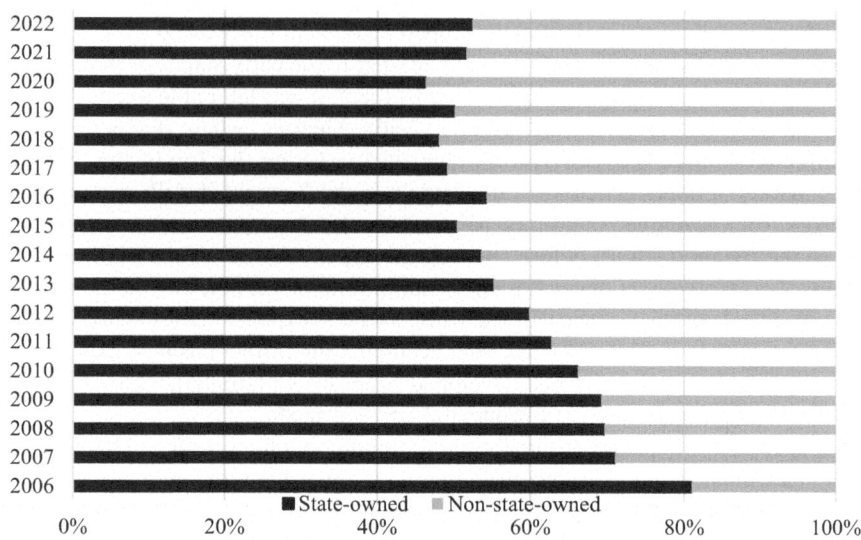

Fig. 3 Distribution of China's non-financial outward FDI stock by registration type of domestic investors. *Source* Ministry of Commerce of the People's Republic of China et al. (2023)

countries, so that the uniqueness of countries can be boiled down to just those differences that cannot be explained by other variables (p. 10). Therefore, this chapter focuses on the framework of the evolutionary stages.

Table 1 shows the three stages of internationalisation of MNEs. An infant MNE is an enterprise taking the first steps towards internationalisation with heavy reliance on exports, modest overseas production in a few countries, and unknown brands. Adolescent MNEs have overseas investments and production in several countries, possibly concentrated in the home region, and own new brands. Mature MNEs operate in most major markets and regions with extensive overseas production, research, and strong global brands.

Below, we discuss the four perspectives in the analytical framework of MNEs evolution presented by Ramamurti (2009, 2020).

4.1 Importance of FSAs

FSAs are capabilities, such as technology, management-related competencies, and access to various management resources, unique to a given enterprise. Successful enterprises abroad have valuable and inimitable FSAs that are considered small MNEs in their infant stage and grow as they evolve.

FSAs are divided into asset and transaction types.

Table 1 Stages of evolution as an MNE

Indicator	Stage 1: infant MNE	Stage 2: adolescent MNE	Stage 3: mature MNE
Importance of FSAs	Low	Low to medium	Medium to high
– Asset-type FSAs (R&D, Brand)	R&D: low Brand: strong at home, unknown abroad	R&D: low to medium Brand: strong at home, up-and-coming abroad	R&D: medium to high Brand: strong global brand
– Transaction-type FSAs	Low	Low to medium	Medium to high
Importance of CSAs	High	High to medium, and falling	Medium to low, and falling
– CAs	High	High to medium, and falling	Medium to low, and falling
– GCAs	High	High to medium, and falling	Medium to low, and falling
Ratio of exports to overseas production	Exports exceed overseas production	Exports and overseas production in balance	Overseas production exceeds exports
Geographic footprint	Few countries, many in home region	Several countries, with emphasis on home region	Dozens of countries, in all major regions

Source Made by author with modifications of Ramamurti (2009, p. 420)

Asset-type FSAs indicate that an enterprise has privileged access to physical facilities, intellectual property, and tangible and intangible resources, including employee knowledge and access to financial capital (Collinson et al. 2020).

Transaction-type FSAs are associated with efficient transactions. Enterprises can generate income because they know how to organise themselves efficiently, both within the country and internationally. They are complementary to asset-type FSAs. If an enterprise wants to be a successful MNE, it must know how to develop an organisational structure that allows it to benefit from the synergies of operations in more than one country (Collinson et al. 2020).

4.2 Importance of CSAs

Even if enterprises lack FSAs, they can expand abroad by utilising CSAs. CSAs can be divided into comparative advantages (CAs), which are natural qualities that cannot be easily changed or created, such as climate, natural resources, and location, and government-created advantages (GCAs), which governments deliberately bring about to increase a country's international competitiveness. Infant MNEs have small

FSAs and rely on CSAs to expand abroad, but as the enterprise evolves, its reliance on CSAs decreases (Ramamurti 2009, 2020).

4.3 Ratio of Exports to Overseas Production

Helpman et al. (2004) analyse the relationship between enterprise productivity and exports/FDI. For exports, enterprises can exploit economies of scale by consolidating their domestic factories. On the one hand, variable costs are higher because they must track transport costs, including tariffs, for exports to foreign countries. In the case of FDI, they do not have to pay tariffs, and transport costs are lower than in the case of exports. On the other hand, fixed costs are higher because at least two factories, one domestic and one foreign local, must be set up and maintained. According to Helpman et al. (2004), the productivity of FDI enterprises exceeds that of exporting enterprises. Therefore, it can be assumed that for MNEs in the infant stage, exports exceed FDI, productivity increases as the enterprise evolves, exports and FDI are at the same level as in the adolescence stage, and FDI exceeds exports in the mature stage.

4.4 Geographic Footprint

In the infant stage, enterprises operate only in a limited number of neighbouring countries/regions; in the adolescent stage, they expand to several neighbouring countries/regions; and in the mature stage, they operate in many major countries/regions. Li (2007) states that most Chinese MNEs lack FSAs and try to utilise CSAs to expand into neighbouring countries/regions rather than globally, implying that many Chinese MNEs are still in their infant stage.

5 Evolution of Lenovo

We provide a brief overview of the Chinese Information and Communication Technology (ICT) enterprise Lenovo before analysing the evolution of Lenovo's internationalisation based on Ramamurti (2009, 2020).

Lenovo was founded in 1984 by 11 members of the Computer Research Institute of the Chinese Academy of Sciences, a business unit of the State Council of China. It started producing its own brand of personal computers (PCs) in 1990 and, with its highly practical technology and services, further increased its market share at low prices. This position has been maintained since then. In February 1994, the enterprise was listed on the Hong Kong Stock Exchange (Xu 2020). In 1996, the enterprise was first in terms of market share in China's PC market and has retained this position since

Evolution of Chinese Information and Communication Technology ...

then. In 1999, Lenovo ranked first among the top 100 electronic information enterprises in China, as published by the Ministry of Electronic Industry (now the Ministry of Industry and Information Industry). Nakagawa (2008) states that Lenovo's success can be attributed, first, to its strategy of following global standards more quickly and more precisely; second, to its orientation towards marketing superiority rather than technological superiority; and third, to its flexible organisational strategy in support of these strategies.

Lenovo started its internationalisation programme in 1988 in Hong Kong (Li 2007). In 2000, Lenovo planned for 20–30% of its sales to come from international markets, but the figure was only 3%, mainly in Southeast Asia. In 2002, the enterprise decided on an internationalisation policy to export PCs to the European market, but withdrew the policy owing to poor sales in the country (Kawai 2008). In December 2004, Lenovo announced the full acquisition of IBM's PC business, taking over all operations of IBM's PC business, including laptop computers and related R&D, production, and sales (Jiang 2020, p. 65). Lenovo's acquisition of IBM's PC business unit was not an extension of its success in the domestic market, but a measure to reverse the stagnation of diversification and internationalisation (Nakagawa 2007). In January 2011, it integrated NEC's PC business; in January 2014, it acquired Motorola Mobile; and in November 2017, it integrated Fujitsu's PC business.

We will now use the framework described in Sect. 4 to analyse Lenovo's evolution as an MNE.

5.1 Importance of FSAs

First, we analysed asset-type FSAs. With the acquisition of IBM, Lenovo acquired more than 10,000 IBM employees and the assets of IBM's PC division. Lenovo also acquired IBM's R&D centres in Yamato, Japan, North Carolina, and USA, through business acquisitions, which significantly increased its R&D capabilities. Moreover, this increased its R&D investment. Lenovo's R&D expenditure-to-revenue ratio increased from 1.1 to 3.5% by 2023 (Fig. 4). In 2005, Lenovo's R&D investments were mainly in the laptop and desktop PC divisions, which increased its R&D capacity. Furthermore, the integration of its business with NEC increased its R&D capacity, enabling it to invest in new areas of R&D, such as tablet PCs and smartphones (Natsume and Lu 2017).

The strengthening of R&D led to brand building and gains in market share. Lenovo was first included in Fortune Global 500 in 2008. It was dropped from the list in 2009 owing to the global financial crisis, but was ranked again in 2011 (449th) and has remained on the list until 2023 (217th) (The Beijing News 2020). The highest ranking was 159th in 2021.

Brand Finance, a UK-based corporate brand valuation consultancy, publishes Brand Finance Global 500, which ranks the world's most valuable corporate brands. Lenovo is ranked every year from 2008 to 2024, with the exception of 2010–2012 (Brand Finance Brandirectly).

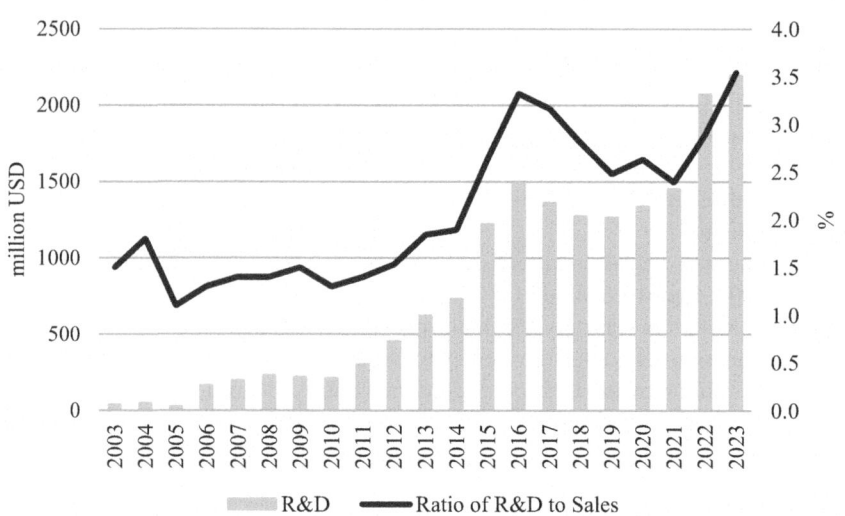

Fig. 4 Lenovo's R&D and ratio of R&D to sales. *Source LENOVO Annual Report* each year edition, Natsume and Lu (2017)

Lenovo has the largest global market share, with 59 million PC shipments in 2023 (Fig. 5). The PC market is expected to continue to grow in 2024, according to IDC (International Data Corporation), as demand is boosted by 'nest egg demand' due to the new coronavirus disaster. PC enterprises aim to increase the demand for artificial intelligence (AI) PCs that can process data at high speeds on their terminals. Lenovo also focussed on the development of high-specification products, including new products, such as PCs with AI semiconductors, at CES, the world's largest technology trade fair, on 8 January 2024 (NIKKEI 2024).

Next, we focus on transaction-type FSAs. In Yuan (2014), as introduced in Sect. 3, social networks, such as human relationships, are considered irregular competitive advantages, which can also be included in FSAs because they are related to the competitive advantage of the enterprise.

Domestically, Lenovo has strong government ties. Lenovo was founded in 1984 by the Chinese Academy of Sciences, a department of the Chinese Government. A core founding member of the enterprise, Liu Denzhi, served as a representative of the National People's Congress, the National Assembly's equivalent, from 1998 to 2013 and as a representative of the National Congress of the Chinese Communist Party, the highest decision-making body of the Party. He had strong connections with political leaders and established a support system for the Chinese government (NIKKEI 2019).

Lenovo also acquires talented people through acquisitions. Lenovo acquired the IBM PC business in 2005. As a part of this transaction, Lenovo and IBM entered a broad-based strategic alliance and partnership. Lenovo capitalised on the brand equity and technology of IBM's ThinkPad to quickly develop various new product lines, such as the Lenovo Yoga for young professionals seeking fun and innovative products,

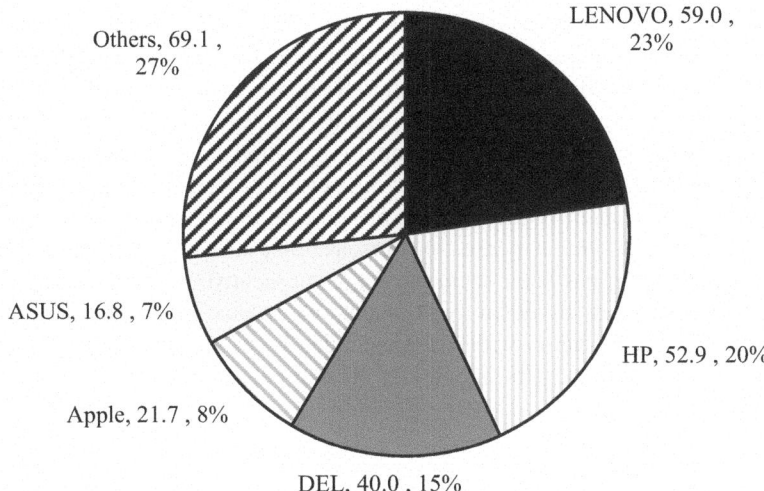

Fig. 5 Top 5 enterprises, worldwide traditional PC shipments and market share in 2023. *Note* Shipments are in millions of units. *Source* IDC

and the Lenovo Z series for small media enterprises seeking reliable computers of good value. The Lenovo-IBM ThinkPad partnership greatly enhanced Lenovo's brand equity and opened a wide range of distribution channels for enterprises. Most importantly, Lenovo not only acquired the ThinkPad production line, but also IBM's management talent, which continues to serve Lenovo (Su et al. 2021).

As described above, Lenovo has built a world-renowned brand, increased its share of the global market for its products, and attracted talented people. Therefore, it can be considered to have reached a mature stage with regard to FSAs.

5.2 Importance of CSAs

The first thing that can be mentioned about CA in China is their large domestic market. While enterprises must have the economies of scale necessary to build a viable production base to become international competitors, the huge domestic markets can be fertile ground for cultivating 'national champions'. Second, China's education and training system supports enterprises by providing them with large numbers of graduates from higher education institutions who are introduced at a low cost (Nölke 2023).

The first GCA is that although Lenovo is a privately owned enterprise, it was originally a state institution. Lenovo's performance declined during the global economic crisis but regained momentum with government support. The largest shareholder of Lenovo's parent enterprise, Legend Holdings Corporation, is the Chinese Academy of Sciences. Although Lenovo is a privately owned enterprise, it has strong links to the state. The second GCA is government policy. China has an abundance of low-wage workers migrating from rural to urban areas due to the existence of a household registration system (Nölke 2023). Outward FDI policies also supported enterprises' overseas expansion regardless of their ownership. For example, the governments of the Zhejiang and Fujian Provinces have strongly supported the multinational management of private enterprises. This simplifies the outward FDI screening and approval processes for private enterprises. They also provide office rent, enterprise setup costs, employee travel, and living expenses to overseas offices (Ohki and Shimizu 2014).

China's population has been declining for 2 consecutive years since 2022, and labour wages have risen significantly in recent years (Jetro Business Briefs 2024). However, it remains a country with a large population. In addition, Lenovo's strong links with the state continue to be maintained. Therefore, its CSAs are still considered to be in the infant stage.

5.3 Ratio of Exports to Overseas Production

In 2012, 91.8% and 87.9% of laptop computers were produced in Asia and China, respectively, whereas 76.5% and 68.2% of desktop computers were produced in Asia and China, respectively (Suehiro 2014), suggesting that high production in Asia results in very large product exports to consumption areas. Recently, Lenovo established local production. In June 2013, a production site was established in North Carolina, USA. Production in the US has the disadvantage of higher labour costs but has the advantage of shorter delivery times (CNET JAPAN 2012). In June 2022, Lenovo opened its first European production site in Budapest, Hungary (NIKKEI 2022). While a large share of Information Technology products is produced in Asian countries, Lenovo is increasing its production in Western countries. TSMC, the world's largest semiconductor contract manufacturer in Taiwan, is currently building semiconductor manufacturing plants in developed countries, such as the US and Japan, and ICT enterprises may increasingly expand into developed countries in the future.

5.4 Geographic Footprint

According to Lenovo's annual report, in 2023, its main subsidiaries will be located in various countries and regions of the world[5] (Table 2). In addition, Lenovo's share of revenue in China since 2006 reached 48.0% in 2010, but then started to decline, reaching 24.0% by 2023 (Fig. 6). However, the share of revenue for 2023 in the US

---

[5] When it comes to manufacturing bases, they are limited to Singapore, India, Switzerland, Japan, and Brazil, in addition to China, and Hungary and the US mentioned above. This is also why the country is judged to be at the infant stage with regard to the export/overseas production ratio.

and Europe was 34.3% and that in the Middle East and Africa was 24.7%, which is higher than the share of revenue in China (Lenovo Group Limited).

From the above, it can be said that Lenovo has reached a mature stage with regard to its geographical presence, as it has subsidiaries in many countries worldwide and generates significant revenue outside China.

The results of this analysis are presented in Table 3. Since FSAs are in the mature stage, CSAs are in the infant stage, the export/overseas production ratio is in the infant stage, and geographical footprints are in the mature stage, Lenovo is collectively considered to have reached the adolescent stage.

6 Conclusion

Based on Ramamurti's (2009, 2020) framework, this chapter analyses the extent to which Lenovo evolved as an MNE. Lenovo's first internationalisation activity was the establishment of Hong Kong Lenovo in 1988, that is, investment in the neighbouring region, which was also characterised by a low amount of R&D and was truly in the infant stage. However, in recent years, Lenovo's evolution as an MNE has been confirmed, as it invests in many countries and regions worldwide, while R&D expenditures have increased, and world-renowned brands have been built.

However, the increasing importance of FSAs does not mean reliance on CSAs is becoming less important. The government's influence on whether enterprises are state or privately owned is significant. Therefore, GCAs may remain strong. If so, Chinese MNEs may remain in the infant stage in the medium to long term with regard to CSAs. In addition, in recent years, the government has begun to restrict outward FDIs because of concerns regarding capital outflows; policies have been issued since the end of 2016 to curb outward FDIs in non-real economic sectors, resulting in a decline in outward FDIs in property, entertainment, and tourism (Tamai 2020).

Regarding the export/overseas production ratio, as mentioned in Sect. 5.3, most PC products are produced in Asia and then exported worldwide. The fragmentation of production processes is increasing, and countries with low technological skills in the ICT industry can manufacture final products by considering only low value-added processes such as product assembly. Therefore, the structure assembly processes will continue to be carried out in low-wage countries and finished products will continue to be transported to places of consumption. In other words, highly productive enterprises in the ICT industry may prefer to produce in low-wage countries and export rather than locally.

Finally, we discuss future research issues. Owing to changes in the business environment caused by the Sino-US conflict and the new Corona disaster, US imports of PCs from China in the first half of 2023 fell by 23.9% y/y. In June 2023, it was reported that Taiwan's Compal Electronics, which reportedly produces laptop PCs for Apple, Dell in the US, Sony in Japan, Asus in Taiwan, and Lenovo in China, would invest USD 260 million to build a production facility in the Lien Ha Thai Industrial Park in Thai Binh Province, northern Vietnam (Akahira 2023). In the future,

Table 2 Principal overseas subsidiaries

Enterprise name	Place	Principal activities
Fujitsu Client Computing Limited	Japan	Manufacturing and distribution of IT products
Lenovo (Australia & New Zealand) Pty Limited	Australia	Distribution of IT products
Lenovo (Belgium) BV	Belgium	Investment holding and distribution of IT products
Lenovo (Canada) Inc	Canada	Distribution of IT products
Lenovo (Danmark) ApS	Denmark	Distribution of IT products
Lenovo (Deutschland) GmbH	Germany	Distribution of IT products
Lenovo Enterprise Solutions (Singapore) Pte. Ltd	Singapore	Manufacturing and wholesaling of computers, computer hardware, and peripheral equipment
Lenovo Enterprise Solutions Ltd	Japan	Distribution of IT products
Lenovo (France) SAS	France	Distribution of IT products
Lenovo (France) SAS	France	Distribution of IT products
Lenovo Global Technology (United States) Inc	USA	Provision of IT services and distribution of IT products
Lenovo (India) Private Limited	India	Manufacturing and distribution of IT products
Lenovo (Israel) Ltd	Israel	Distribution of IT products
Lenovo (Italy) S.r.l	Italy	Distribution of IT products
Lenovo Japan LLC	Japan	Distribution of IT products
Lenovo Korea LLC	Korea	Wholesale and retail trade of computer, peripheral equipment, and software
Lenovo Mexico, S. de R.L. de C.V	Mexico	Distribution of IT products
Lenovo (Schweiz) GmbH	Switzerland	Manufacturing and distribution of IT products
Lenovo (Singapore) Pte. Ltd	Singapore	Manufacturing and wholesaling of computers, computer hardware, and peripheral equipment
Lenovo (South Africa) (Pty) Limited	South Africa	Distribution and marketing of IT products
Lenovo (Spain), S.L	Spain	Distribution of IT products
Lenovo (Sweden) AB	Sweden	Distribution of IT products
Lenovo Technology (United Kingdom) Limited	UK	Distribution of IT products
Lenovo Technology B.V	Netherlands	Distribution of IT products

(continued)

Table 2 (continued)

Enterprise name	Place	Principal activities
Lenovo Technology Sdn. Bhd	Malaysia	Retail sale of computers, computer equipment, and supplies
Lenovo Tecnologia (Brasil) Ltda	Brazil	Manufacturing and distribution of IT products
Lenovo (Thailand) Limited	Thailand	Distribution of IT products as well as mobile phone, smartphone and tablet, server, and storage
Lenovo (United States) Inc	USA	Distribution of IT products
Lenovo (Venezuela), SA	Venezuela	Distribution of IT products
Medion AG	Germany	Retail and service business for consumer electronic products and complementary digital services
Motorola Mobility Comércio de Produtos Eletronicos Ltda	Brazil	Distribution of communication products, developer, owner, licensor, and seller of communications hardware and software
Motorola Mobility International Sales LLC	USA	Holding company
Motorola Mobility LLC	USA	Developer, owner, licensor, and seller of communications hardware and software
NEC Personal Computers, Ltd	Japan	Manufacturing and distribution of IT products
Shimane Fujitsu Limited	Japan	Manufacturing and distribution of IT products
Stoneware, Inc	USA	Development and distribution of IT products
Edgebricks Pte. Limited	Singapore	Development of software and applications

Note This table includes the principal overseas subsidiaries held directly or indirectly by the Lenovo Group, which are significant to the results of the year or form a substantial portion of the group's net assets
Source LENOVO 2022/23 Annual Report

the analysis of Chinese MNEs will increasingly need to consider not only exports from China to consuming countries or the expansion of Chinese enterprises into consuming countries but also bypass exports and outsourcing to other enterprises.

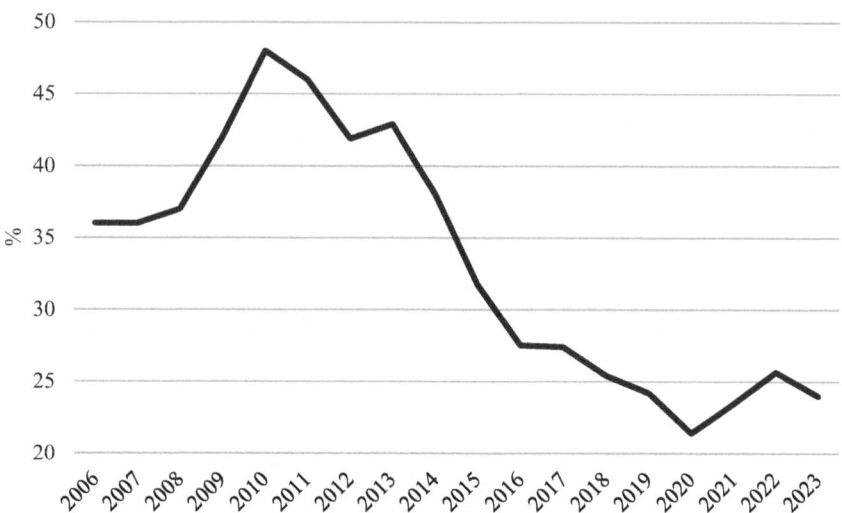

Fig. 6 Share of Lenovo's revenue in China to total. *Source LENOVO Annual Report* each year edition, Natsume and Lu (2017)

Table 3 The evolution of LENOVO as an MNE

Indicator	Level	Stage as an MNE
Importance of firm-specific advantages (FSAs)	Medium to high	Mature
– Asset-type FSAs (R&D, Brand)	R&D: medium to high Brand: strong global brand	Mature
– Transaction-type FSAs	Medium to high	Mature
Importance of home-country specific advantages (CSAs)	High	Infant
Ratio of exports to overseas production	Exports exceed overseas production	Infant
Geographic footprint	Dozens of countries, in all major regions	Mature

Source Made by author

Acknowledgements This research was supported by the JSPS KAKENHI Fund for the Promotion of Joint International Research (Fostering Joint International Research (B), 22KK0023 entitled *International joint research for the construction of emerging MNC theory and the analysis of changes in the international division of labour*, grant-in-aid of the project-based collaborative research for the AY 2022 entitled *Comparative research on Slavic-Eurasian and Asian multinationals and the structural changes in the international division of labour* provided by the Slavic-Eurasian Research Centre, Hokkaido University, Japan and Special Research Grant 2024, Matsuyama University, Japan.

The author is indebted to Professor Emeritus Ravi Ramamurti (Northeastern University), Professor Emeritus Shinichiro Tabata (Hokkaido University), and Professor Emeritus Keiji Natsume

(Ryukoku University) for their useful suggestions and constructive feedback on the earlier drafts of this research.

References

Akahira H (2023) Impact of the US-China conflict on the supply chain to the US: signs of change in telecommunications equipment. Overseas Business Information, 16th October, 2023. https://www.jetro.go.jp/biz/areareports/special/2023/0904/299f5f4e8cb02b20.html (in Japanese)

Brand Finance Brandirectly, Global 500 Ranking. https://brandirectory.com/rankings/global

Buckley PJ, Casson M (1991) The future of the multinational enterprise, 2nd edn. The Macmillan Press

Collinson S, Narula R, Rugman AM (2020) International business, 8th edn. Pearson

CNET JAPAN (2012) Lenovo manufactures PCs in the US: ask the executive about the benefits. 19th October, 2012. https://japan.cnet.com/article/35023176/ (in Japanese)

Dunning JH (1979) Explaining changing patterns of international production: In defence of the electic theory. Oxford Bull Econ Stat 41(4):269–295

Helpman E, Melitz MJ, Yeaple SR (2004) Export versus FDI with heterogeneous firms. Am Econ Rev 94(1):300–316

Hymer SH (1976) The international operations of national firms: a study of direct foreign investment. MIT Press, Cambridge, Mass

IDC (2024) Worldwide PC shipments declined 2.7% year over year in the fourth quarter of 2023 but visions of growth lie ahead, According to IDC. IDC, 10th January, 2024. https://www.idc.com/getdoc.jsp?containerId=prUS51753924

Jetro Business Briefs (2024) China's population declined for the second year in a row, with the number of births reaching a new low. 29th January, 2024. https://www.jetro.go.jp/biznews/2024/01/766b6a6925e4a768.html (in Japanese)

Jiang H (2020) Strategic asset acquisition and chinese outward FDI. KOYO SHOBO (in Japanese)

Kang R (2013) Comparison of overseas development of Chinese and Japanese enterprises. In: Kawai S (ed) Overseas management of Chinese multinationals: with a focus on East Asian manufacturing. Nippon Hyoron sha, pp 15–36 (in Japanese)

Kawai S (2008) International competitive strategies of Chinese enterprises: comparative analysis of haier and lenovo. In: Takahashi (ed) Chinese economy expanding overseas. Nippon Hyoron sha, pp 164–183 (in Japanese)

Lenovo Group Limited, Annual Report each year edition

Li PP (2007) Toward an integrated theory of multinational evolution: the evidence of Chinese multinational enterprises as latecomers. J Int Manag 13:296–318

Liu Y (2014) The internationalization strategy of Chinese multinational firms: focusing on the ZTE Co Ltd. Case. J Bus Adm 83:63–78 (in Japanese)

Marukawa T (2008) Multinational enterprises from China. In: Marukawa T, Nakagawa R (eds) Multinational enterprises from China. Doyukan, pp 1–20 (in Japanese)

Ministry of Commerce of the People's Republic of China, National Bureau of Statistics, State Administration of Foreign Exchange (2023) 2022 Statistical bulletin of china's outward foreign direct investment. China Commerce and Trade Press

Nakagawa R (2017) The development of multinationalisation of Chinese enterprises and its implications: a proposal of middle-income state multinationals. J Bus Stud 57(1):33–44 (in Japanese)

Nakagawa R (2007) Chinese IT industry. Minerva Shobo (in Japanese)

Nakagawa R (2008) Huawei and Lenovo. In: Marukawa T, Nakagawa R (eds) Multinational enterprises from China. Doyukan, pp 69–96 (in Japanese)

Natsume K, Lu Y (2017) ICT multinationals in modern China. Bunshindo Publishing Corporation (in Japanese)

NIKKEI (2019) Lenovo founder Liu retires, acquires IBM business to make it a global enterprise. 18th December, 2019 (in Japanese)

NIKKEI (2022) Lenovo opens its first European own production site in Hungary. 24th June, 2022 (in Japanese)

NIKKEI (2024) Global shipments of personal computers in 2023 to fall by 13.9%, the second consecutive year of decline. 11th January, 2024 (in Japanese)

Nölke A (2023) Second image IPE: bridging the gap between comparative and international political economy. Palgrave Macmillan.

Ohki H, Shimizu K (2014) Internationalization strategies of Chinese enterprises. JETRO (in Japanese)

Ramamurti R (2020) Analytical misunderstandings about emerging-market multinationals. J Comp Econ Stud 15:9–20

Ramamurti R (2009) What have we learned about emerging-market MNEs? In: Ramamurti R, Singh JV (eds) Emerging multinationals in emerging markets. Cambridge University Press

Rugman AM, Nguen QTK (2014) Modern international business theory and emerging market multinational companies. In: Cuervo-Cazurra A, Ramamurti R (eds) Understanding multinationals from emerging markets. Cambridge University Press, pp 53–80

Su M, Shi LH, Zhao M, Tan K (2021) Emerging dragons: how do Chinese companies expand overseas? In: Wu T, Bu N (eds) International business in the new Asia-Pacific: strategies, opportunities and threats. Springer

Suehiro A (2014) Newly emerging Asian Economies: beyond the catch-up. Iwanami Publisher (in Japanese)

Tamai Y (2020) The transformation of China's outward FDI. Mizuho Insight, 4th March, pp 1–10 (in Japanese)

The Beijing News (2020) Lenovo ranked 224th in the fortune global 500 for the 10th consecutive year. 10th August 2020. https://baijiahao.baidu.com/s?id=1674646183062883155&wfr=spider&for=pc (in Chinese)

UNCTAD (2006) World investment report 2006: FDI from developing and transition economies: implications for development. https://unctad.org/system/files/official-document/wir2006_en.pdf

Vernon R (1966) International investment and international trade in the product cycle. Quart J Econ 80:190–207

Xu F (2020) Chinese global enterprises' actual situation. Chikura Publishing Company (in Japanese)

Yuan Z (2014) The frontier of Chinese firms' OFDI: expansion and development of multinationals from developing countries into Asia. Soseisha (in Japanese)

Yuan Z (2023) Chinese multinationals expanding globally. Soseisha (in Japanese)

Takuma Kobayashi is an associate professor in the Faculty of Economics at Matsuyama University (Japan). He received his Ph.D. in Economics from Kyoto University (Japan). His main interests include the Chinese economy, international economics, and development economics. His publications include the following: Kobayashi, T. (2023) "Will Japanese Enterprises Leave China?" *Letters of Economic Science*, No. 157, pp. 2-6 (in Japanese), Kobayashi, T. (2022) "China's Economic System with Strong Government Influence: Consideration of Government-Enterprise Relations" in S. Mizobata (ed.), *Economics of State-led Capitalism*, Bunshindo, pp. 224–248 (in Japanese), Kobayashi, T. (2017) "Overcapacity in China after Economic Crisis: In Relation to Industrial Location", *The Journal of Comparative Economic Studies*, Vol. 12, pp. 143–160.

Internationalisation Strategies of Russian Financial Multinationals: From Global Expansion to Global Market Exodus?

Victor Gorshkov

Abstract In this chapter, we applied the modified framework of the evolution as a financial MNE suggested by Ramamurti to the case of the largest Russian state-owned bank, *Sberbank*, which has actively pursued internationalisation since 2011. The results of our analysis demonstrate that *Sberbank* has benefited significantly from globalisation and Russia's integration into the world economy to evolve from an inefficient state-owned bank established at the launch of Russia's market transition to Russia's leading state-owned multinational bank. We conclude that despite the fact that *Sberbank* possessed medium-to-high levels of bank-specific advantages in Eastern and Central Europe, it remained predominantly a regional financial multinational, as measured by the depth and breadth of its internationalisation, even at its peak. Thus, despite some limitations in the assessment methodology, *Sberbank* is a representative case of an adolescent financial multinational. Russia's new reality of global isolation from Western financial markets is pushing its banks to find new markets in friendly jurisdictions such as China, India, and the United Arab Emirates. However, foreign entry into these markets is hindered by high entry costs, administrative and regulatory restrictions, and the increased risk of secondary sanctions on counterparties. Consequently, the future internationalisation strategies of Russian banks remain uncertain.

Keywords Russian multinationals · Internationalisation strategies · Stage of evolution · Bank-specific advantages · Impact of sanctions

1 Introduction

The international presence of Russian financial multinational enterprises (henceforth Russian financial MNEs) sharply curtailed after the deterioration of the geopolitical environment between Russia and Ukraine in February 2022. In 2013, at the peak of the foreign expansion of Russian financial MNEs, Russian banks had 6 branches,

V. Gorshkov (✉)
Faculty of International Economic Studies, University of Niigata Prefecture, Niigata, Japan
e-mail: vgorshkov@unii.ac.jp

58 subsidiaries, and 51 representative offices abroad (Abalkina 2014; Abalkina and Ivanova 2014), while currently, there remains only 4 branches and 19 representative offices. Therefore, the cases of successful rapid foreign expansion witnessed in mid-2012 were short-lived due to the imposition of economic and financial sanctions on Russia in 2014 and 2022. In particular, two state-owned financial MNEs, *Sberbank* and *VTB,* which had the largest international presence, were forced to withdraw their businesses from the European market in 2022 and bore significant losses as a result. This put an end to the era of massive foreign expansion for Russian financial MNEs, which had intensified in the mid-2000s.

In response, many Russian financial MNEs have publicly announced their plans to pivot to the markets of the so-called 'friendly countries' such as China and India. *Sberbank* declared in June 2023 that it had obtained permission to open a second branch in Mumbai, and a year earlier, it had also revealed plans to open a branch in Beijing, which already has a representative office. Moreover, China seems to be an attractive destination for many other Russian banks, for example, *Alfa-bank* and *Rosbank,* which have also been considering entry into this market (Uvarchev 2023). The question of whether this change in internationalisation strategies is feasible remains of great interest to academics, businesspeople, and policymakers.

The internationalisation strategies of Russian financial MNEs have been a research subject for many Russian and foreign scholars (Gorshkov 2013; Panibratov 2010; Panibratov 2013; Panibratov 2016; Abalkina 2010; Abalkina 2014; Abalkina and Ivanova 2014; Nikitina and Volkova 2016; Larioshina 2019; Panibratov and Verba 2011). Numerous studies have focussed on the evolution of the foreign expansion of Russian financial MNEs, their motives, modes, organisational forms, and strategies when entering foreign markets. Most of these studies are descriptive in nature and formulate conclusions based on the examination of case studies of specific banks and their internationalisation strategies within the existing theories of international business (IB) and multinational banking.

Consequently, their conclusions are straightforward and can be summarised in a few central arguments. First, Russian financial MNEs do not possess any significant competitive advantages in the markets of developed countries. Second, their expansion abroad is driven by the geographical, historical, cultural, and institutional proximity of host country markets to Russia, thus limiting their success to markets such as the Commonwealth of Independent States (CIS) region, which are less developed. Third, the foreign direct investment (FDI) motives of Russian financial MNEs include serving Russian clients engaged in bilateral trade between Russia and host countries or channelling cheap financing from international capital markets needed by Russian companies engaged in foreign trade and IB.

Thus, previous research fails to accurately explain whether Russian financial MNEs possess firm-specific advantages (FSAs) that allow them to compete effectively in host country markets. In addition, the existing IB theories applied to the cases of Russian financial MNEs often provide static snapshots of reality and compare Russian financial MNEs with MNEs from developed countries. Consequently, they fail to recognise the notion of the evolution of a financial MNE and its ability to nurture and acquire the capabilities necessary for fostering FSAs as sources of new competitive advantages.

The purpose of this chapter is twofold. First, by modifying the existing framework of the evolution of MNEs suggested by Ramamurti (2009, 2016, 2020) to apply to the cases of Russian financial MNEs, we reconsider the evolution and internationalisation strategies of Russian financial MNEs. In particular, we identify the extent to which the foreign expansion of Russian financial MNEs can be attributed to their possession of FSAs, compared to the role played by home country-specific advantages (CSAs) and government-created advantages (GCAs). This knowledge will help in assessing the developmental stage of Russian financial MNEs in the framework suggested by Ramamurti (2009, 2016, 2020), that is, whether they represent cases of infant, adolescent, or mature MNEs.

Second, we depict major changes in the internationalisation strategies of Russian financial MNEs and assess the extent to which Russian financial MNEs remain resilient to economic and financial sanctions. In particular, we aim to highlight the challenges and limitations of the reorientation towards new foreign markets in friendly jurisdictions, such as China, India, and the United Arab Emirates.

Sberbank, the largest state-owned bank among Russian financial MNEs, was selected as the case study. This bank was selected because alone it constitutes approximately 31% of the total assets of Russia's banking system and provides 32% of all corporate loans (including 46% of loans to small and medium enterprises) and 37.7% of retail loans (Sberbank 2023). In addition, it was the bank with the largest number of foreign affiliates at the peak of foreign expansion in 2013 and had an extensive network of business transactions in approximately 22 countries in 2021. Lastly, *Sberbank* is the only Russian financial MNE that has rapidly improved its position in the *Fortune Global 500*; it joined the ranking in 2007 in 406th place, peaked in 2015 in 177th place, and landed in the 270th place in 2022.

2 Theoretical Background on the Internationalisation of Financial MNEs

A financial MNE is a multinational enterprise operating in the financial sector that includes banks, insurance companies, and investment firms. Financial MNEs operate in multiple countries and provide a wide range of financial services to corporate and retail customers.

Internationalisation theories of financial MNEs have evolved from the IB theories of internationalisation initially developed for non-financial MNEs and later complemented by theories of internationalisation pertinent to financial MNEs.

Previous research has shown that financial MNEs have unique patterns of internationalisation. Financial services are intangible and indispensable to banking activities, are based on trust, and possess high levels of transaction and currency risks. In addition, financial MNEs provide a wide range of financial services for both retail and corporate clients; thus, the internationalisation strategy significantly depends on the target clients (Nikitina and Volkova 2016). Moreover, the financial industry is highly regulated in many countries, thus resulting in the choice of internationalisation strategy being highly predetermined by the institutional environments of both the home and host countries. While recognising these peculiarities of financial MNEs, we nevertheless argue that internationalisation strategies pertinent to financial MNEs in a broader sense represent subtypes of the FDI motives conventionally applied to examining the internationalisation strategies of non-financial MNEs.

Conventionally, the internationalisation of non-financial firms has been analysed using John Dunning's eclectic paradigm (Ownership-Location-Internalisation: OLI paradigm), which was formulated based on the theories of transaction costs, internalisation, international trade, and factors of production. This approach remains the cornerstone of IB research on the motives and strategies for internationalisation. Ownership advantages (O) were later labelled FSAs. Scholars of the resource-based view (RBV) extended the discussion further by highlighting the importance of a firm's current resources and capabilities (tangible and intangible) and those that it aims to acquire via internationalisation. A recent contribution of the RBV is the theory of dynamic capabilities proposed by Teece et al. (1997), which refers to an organisation's capability to adapt, innovate, and reconfigure its resources and capabilities to sustain its competitive advantage in a rapidly changing external environment.

Contemporary IB theory is rooted in the idea that a firm's internationalisation strategy is formulated based on the effective evaluation of FSAs (asset-type, transaction-type, and recombinant FSAs) and the location-specific advantages (LSAs) of the host country (Collinson et al. 2020). In addition, the role of the home country's CSAs and GCAs has been highlighted, particularly in the case of emerging market multinationals (Ramamurti 2020). The most common FDI motives among non-financial firms are market-seeking FDI, resource-seeking FDI, efficiency-seeking FDI (internalisation strategy), and strategic asset-seeking FDI.

The aforementioned theories, with some limitations and extensions, can be applied to examining the internationalisation of financial MNEs. For instance, peculiar internationalisation strategies of banks, such as the application of competitive advantages, follow-the-customer, leadership (banks penetrate foreign markets first and then bring their customers from the home country), and follow-the-leader summarised in Nikitina and Volkova (2016), are simply specific cases of market-seeking FDI by financial MNEs. The primary objective in these cases is to make use of the untapped opportunities in foreign markets, regardless of whether these opportunities have been created by foreign or domestic clients. Likewise, capital procurement in international capital markets can be regarded as a specific case of resource-seeking FDI, while the diversification of risks, the institutional strategy of foreign expansion (entering markets with attractive and high-quality institutions), and foreign expansion into markets with low cultural distance (cultural proximity) can equally be explained as cases for improving the overall efficiency of financial MNEs via internalisation, and thus, with some limitations, represent cases of efficiency-seeking FDI. Finally, strategic asset-seeking motives can explain the acquisition of banks by emerging market financial MNEs in developed and other developing countries, establishing an international presence in global financial sectors, and gaining access to the advantages of global financial markets and institutions.

Another strand of literature worth mentioning is research on the internationalisation of emerging market multinationals that provides evidence that emerging market MNEs utilise peculiar patterns of internationalisation that are sometimes different from developed country MNEs. For instance, the *linkage, leverage and learning perspective (LLL perspective)* suggested by Mathews (2017) refers to the idea that emerging market MNEs sometimes pursue *accelerated internationalisation* through connecting and making use of technology-rich companies or companies already active in targeted markets *(linkage)*, gaining access to technologies and/or market position and/or resources that lie outside the emerging MNE and can be incorporated into it *(leverage)*, and repeated application of linkage and leverage *(learning)*. Another theory, the *springboard perspective*, highlights the strategic use of foreign subsidiaries or operations as a springboard for expanding into other markets, and recognises that establishing a presence in a foreign market can provide a platform for accessing adjacent markets and markets with low cultural, administrative, geographical, or economic distance (Luo and Tung 2007). However, the application of these perspectives to financial MNEs is somewhat limited, as financial markets are highly regulated in most countries with significant regulatory differences among them.

Ramamurti (2020) contributed significantly to the advancement of internationalisation theory and highlighted major theoretical misunderstandings about emerging market MNEs. He suggested avoiding a simple comparison of the 'nationality' of MNEs and aiming instead to find variables that could be used analytically to explain differences in internationalisation across different countries. He also highlighted that emerging market MNEs have different FSAs from developed country MNEs and stressed the importance of analysing the evolutionary stages of an MNE (infant, adolescent, and mature MNE). In addition, Ramamurti suggested analysing the global context under which MNEs internationalised and distinguishing between CSAs (natural resource endowments, comparative advantages of a country) and GCAs (creation of complementary assets by investing in physical infrastructure, economic infrastructure, human capital development, industrial policies, and international agreements). However, Ramamurti's (2009, 2016, 2020) framework of the evolution as an MNE was developed to examine non-financial MNEs from emerging markets. Recent studies have highlighted the importance of widening the concept of transnationality to consider companies with a low portfolio of fixed assets abroad, such as digital and financial companies, and companies internationalising via non-equity entry modes (Ietto-Gillies 2022).

3 Internationalisation of Russia's Banking Sector in 1990–2022

The evolution of the foreign expansion of Russian banks can be divided, conditionally, into the historical periods listed in Table 1.

In the 1990s, newly established private banks sought opportunities to establish correspondent relations with foreign financial institutions and developed their networks by primarily establishing representative offices in host countries, as this minimised entry costs for Russian banks. The purpose of the representative offices was to conduct market research on the financial industries of their host countries and to assist Russian clients in establishing the business contacts necessary to conduct foreign trade transactions. By September 1995, Russian financial institutions had established 110 representative offices in 46 countries, covering almost all the regions of the world. The largest number of representative offices were established in the United Kingdom (12) and Germany (11). By 1997, the number of representative offices increased to 147, of which 112 were located in non-CIS countries. In 1997, 22 branches and approximately 10 subsidiaries were registered abroad (e.g. *VTB* in Cyprus, *Stolichny Bank* in the Netherlands, *Alfa-bank* in Kazakhstan). Russian banks expanded primarily through greenfield FDI, with a few cases of M&A. Many banks established foreign affiliates in Cyprus, as there were lax regulations at the time, and there were also a few banks in the former USSR republics, namely, Belarus, Ukraine, Kazakhstan, and Latvia. However, the internationalisation of the banking sector of this period was not sustainable and halted after the 1998 financial crisis (Abalkina 2014).

In 2000–2009, Russian banks launched a new wave of foreign expansion primarily into neighbouring CIS countries: *Sberbank* acquired domestic banks in Ukraine and Kazakhstan, and *VTB* entered the markets of Azerbaijan, Armenia, Georgia, Belarus, and Ukraine. *Bank of Moscow* established a subsidiary in Ukraine in 2005. Thus, in contrast to the 1990s, Russian banks prioritised brownfield FDI as the mode of entry into foreign markets during this period. There were approximately 40–50 representative offices (one-third of the newly established offices was registered in the CIS), 6 branches, and 58 subsidiaries. The improved capitalisation levels of Russian banks in this period provided further opportunities to penetrate foreign markets and meet the growing demand for Russian MNEs operating in the CIS region (Abalkina 2014; Abalkina and Ivanova 2014). The FDI motives for expanding into the CIS region include market-seeking FDI (growing markets in the CIS with increased demand for banking services; follow-the-customer, such as servicing Russian MNEs operating in the region) and resource-seeking FDI (acquisition of under-evaluated assets in CIS banking markets). Due to the cultural and geographic proximity, and common experience of market transition reforms and the superior quality of Russia's institutions in comparison to less mature CIS markets, it is reasonable to assume that Russian banks possessed competitive advantages (transaction-type FSAs) in this region.

Table 1 The evolution of foreign expansion of Russian banks

Period	Targeted host countries (regions)	Motives and strategies of internationalisation	Entry modes	Organisational forms	Number of foreign affiliates established/closed
1990–1999	Western Europe CIS countries Former USSR republics	establishment of correspondent relations with foreign banks; market research; banks formed under financial industrial groups	Mostly greenfield; a few cases of M&A	Representative offices	1997: 147 representative offices (76% in non-CIS countries) 22 branches, 10 subsidiaries
2000–2009	CIS Western Europe Eastern Europe Asia	CIS: market-seeking FDI (growing markets in CIS with increased demand for banking services; follow-the-customer); resource-seeking FDI (acquisition of under-evaluated assets in CIS); transaction-type FSAs (cultural, geographic proximity, common experience of market transition reforms)	Brownfield FDI	Subsidiaries	2009: 44 representative offices (30% in Western Europe, 30% in CIS) 6 branches 58 subsidiaries
2010–2013	Eastern Europe Western Europe Middle East (Turkey)	Eastern Europe: market-seeking FDI (follow-the-customer; retail and corporate clients in Europe); strategic asset-seeking (international presence in Europe; acquisition of an established banking network) Middle East: market-seeking FDI	Brownfield FDI	Subsidiaries	2013: 51 representative offices (33% in CIS, 27%—Western Europe, 24%—Eastern Europe)

(continued)

Table 1 (continued)

Period	Targeted host countries (regions)	Motives and strategies of internationalisation	Entry modes	Organisational forms	Number of foreign affiliates established/closed
2014–2021	Western Europe (Germany)	Market-seeking FDI (online banking) gradual downsizing due to economic and financial sanctions	Greenfield FDI	Subsidiary	n/a gradual downsizing of activities. Sberbank withdrew from Turkey and announces plans to leave other markets
2022–nowadays	Asia (China, India) Middle East (United Arab Emirates)	Sanctions-resilience strategy	Greenfield FDI	Branches	2023: 4 branches (India, China, Cyprus (under liquidation) 19 representative offices (Uzbekistan, Italy, Armenia, Venezuela, Iran, Kyrgyzstan, India, Mongolia, China)

Source Made by author with references to Abalkina (2014), Abalkina and Ivanova (2014), Uvarchev (2023), and reports and news

In addition, during this period, the foreign network of banks established during the USSR to service foreign trade, investment, and capital financing transactions with foreign countries was transferred to *VTB*. Thus, *VTB* automatically gained an international presence in Austria (2005), Germany (2005), France (2005), and the United Kingdom (2005). It then expanded into Angola in 2006. Foreign expansion of Russian banks continued during the global financial crisis of 2007–2008: *VTB* established branches in China (2008) and India (2008) (Abalkina and Ivanova 2014).

In 2010–2013, Russian banks actively penetrated non-CIS countries, with the most active players being banks with state capital participation, namely, *Sberbank*, *VTB*, and *Gazprombank*. *VTB* entered the Serbian market (2013), while *Sberbank* entered Switzerland (2011) via M&A and acquired *Denizbank* (Turkey) and *Volksbank* (Austria) in 2012 for 3.5 billion USD and 0.5 billion USD, respectively (Abalkina 2014). *Volksbank* had an extensive presence in the Slovak Republic, Czech Republic, Hungary, Slovenia, Croatia, Bosnia, and Herzegovina, thus ensuring market access to Eastern and Central Europe for *Sberbank*. The FDI motives for expanding into Eastern Europe included market-seeking FDI (follow-the-customer; serving retail and corporate clients in Europe) and strategic asset-seeking (international presence in Europe; acquisition of established banking networks with a customer base). As for the case of *Denizbank*, this remains the largest M&A acquisition by a Russian bank; *Sberbank* entered the Turkish market for multiple reasons, such as the growing profit potential of the market, geographical proximity, planned large infrastructural projects, and to develop a retail business in the country. *Denizbank* had a large domestic branch and ATM network which was further fortified by *Sberbank* (Larioshina 2019).

In 2014–2021, there was only one subsidiary established abroad. In 2014, *Sberbank Europe* (Austria) received a syndicated loan of 350 million euros and launched *Sberbank Direct* (Germany), an online direct bank offering basic retail products. *Sberbank Direct* collected 1.7 billion euros by 2015 and launched an online instant loan offer in 2018. Thus, the internationalisation motives of this bank can be explained by market-seeking FDI (serving retail customers).

In 2016, economic and financial sanctions imposed on Russian banks by the United States and the EU after the annexation of Crimea forced *Sberbank* to sell its subsidiaries in Slovenia, Ukraine in 2017, and Turkey in 2019. It also planned to sell its subsidiaries in Bosnia and Herzegovina, Croatia, and Hungary in 2021, but these deals were not finalised. Other banks refrained from further foreign expansion. In December 2017, *VTB Bank (Europe) SE* was established in Frankfurt by merging *VTB Bank (Austria) AG*, *VTB Bank (Deutschland) AG*, and *VTB Bank (France)* under the massive restructuring of *VTB*'s assets in Europe. The newly established subsidiary had a branch in Vienna and an online retail platform, the *VTB Direktbank*.

The massive foreign market exodus of Russian banks began in 2022, following the geopolitical developments between Russia and Ukraine. Correspondent accounts of *Sberbank* were sanctioned and later operations with *Sberbank* were blocked by the United States, EU, United Kingdom, and Switzerland. After the imposition of sanctions, the European Central Bank announced that *Sberbank's* subsidiaries in Bosnia and Herzegovina, Croatia, and Hungary had significant problems with deposit outflows and faced the possibility of going bankrupt. In March 2022, *Sberbank Europe AG* was prohibited from conducting further operations, and shares of its subsidiaries in Croatia and Slovenia were transferred to local banks. Nevertheless, *Sberbank* managed to sell its subsidiaries in Serbia, Switzerland, and Kazakhstan (RBK News 16 June 2023). In 2022, *Sberbank* bore 143.3 billion RUB of losses due to the exodus from its European markets. In June 2023, *Sberbank* announced that it had sold *Sberbank Europe AG* to an Austrian company, thus ending its presence in Europe. *VTB* also lost control over its *VTB (Europe) SE*, as its assets were frozen and it was liquidated and reopened under a new name, *OWH SE*. The total losses for *VTB* from the loss of *VTB Bank Europe* and *VTB Capital* in London were estimated at 209 billion RUB (Batyrov 2023).

Previous research has shown that only the largest, financially stable, and profitable Russian banks had established an international presence because foreign markets, particularly in Europe and the USA, are highly competitive and concentrated, and foreign market entry costs remain a burden for the majority of Russian banks with miniscule levels of capitalisation (Gorshkov 2013; Abalkina 2010, 2014). Regarding internationalisation strategies, previous studies (for instance, Abalkina and Ivanova 2014) have demonstrated that Russian financial MNEs do not possess significant competitive advantages (bank-specific advantages) and penetrate non-CIS markets to follow their customers and establish settlement transactions, to serve foreign trade and investment transactions between Russia and the host country, or to procure financial capital. FDI motives for expanding into CIS countries include, conventionally, cultural, geographical, and institutional proximity of these markets to Russia, and the common legacy of market transitions (Abalkina 2010, 2014; Abalkina and Ivanova 2014; Gorshkov 2013; Panibratov 2010).

4 Sberbank: A Short Overview of the Development Path from a State-Owned Inefficient Giant to an Emerging MNE

In post-Soviet Russia, *Sberbank* (the successor of the Savings Bank of the Russian Soviet Federative Socialist Republic) was the largest universal bank despite the establishment of numerous private and other state-owned commercial banks. Until 2007, the bank had a very low level of trust among its customers; its operations were extremely time-consuming and inefficient, and favouritism and nepotism were prevalent in the provision of loans. In summary, *Sberbank* was perceived as an inefficient state giant by the majority of the population.

Since 2007, when Herman Gref, the former Minister of Economic Development, was appointed chairman of *Sberbank*, the bank has pursued a customer-oriented style of management and effectively adopted global standards of corporate social responsibility (CSR) and environmental, social, and corporate governance (ESG). Since his appointment, Gref has effectively incorporated Western-style (IBM's market of ideas) and Asian-style management practices (*kaizen* and *Toyota's 5 S*), frequently consulted with world-famous consulting agencies and promoted corporate governance reforms (Karasyuk 2014). All these measures eventually enabled *Sberbank* to become the first Russian financial MNE to join *Fortune's Global 500* ranking of the world's leading companies. In 2010, the bank launched a system of direct online banking and established *SberBank Online* in 2011, indicating its gradual shift towards *bank 3.0*, a banking system based on the Internet and online services rather than solely on the network of branches and ATMs.

Since the first round of sanctions in 2014, *Sberbank* sought opportunities for domestic growth, and by correctly grasping structural changes in the global banking industry towards digitalisation, it initiated a shift to actively adopting digital technologies (Internet banking, and *bank 4.0*—utilisation of artificial intelligence (AI) and construction of an original digital ecosystem). In 2020, *Sberbank* launched a rebranding campaign, updated its name to *Sber* and began positioning itself as a technological company. *Sber* acquired e-commerce and other related businesses such as food delivery, mortgages, media, entertainment, and taxi services. The bank was able to successfully develop innovations in partnerships with Western (mostly US) companies. In 2021, *Sberbank's* non-financial profits accounted for approximately 1.1% of its total profits, according to its annual report.

Corporate reforms coincided with the internationalisation strategy that *Sberbank* launched in 2011, which is described in detail in Sect. 6. The combined positive impact of corporate governance reforms, internationalisation strategies, and digitisation led to an outstanding improvement in *Sberbank*'s ranking in *Fortune's Global 500*, which ranked it 157th in 2015, and an international presence in as many as 22 countries by 2021.

In short, three factors contributed significantly to the successful transformation of *Sberbank* from an inefficient state-owned giant to an emerging MNE: effective corporate reforms to introduce global standards of CSR, digitisation of its business, and the implementation of an internationalisation strategy. Among the three, its digitisation and internationalisation strategies have proved to be the most vulnerable areas and have been hit the most after the imposition of economic sanctions: *Sberbank* has had to sell some of its non-financial businesses that form part of its digital ecosystem and withdraw from the European and a few CIS markets.

Sberbank's B2C ecosystem is comprised of 106.7 million clients, with the daily active users of its *SberBank Online* service numbering at 40.9 million in 2022. Its financial services include the provision of loans (53.8% market share in mortgage loans, 37.7% in retail loans), a banking card business (137 million debit cards and 17.8 million credit cards issued, 46.4% market share in credit card issuance), as well as insurance and brokerage services (19.1% in brokerage services). Its non-financial businesses have been reduced to e-commerce, entertainment, foodtech and mobility, and health because of the sanctions.

The B2B ecosystem comprises more than three million corporate customers, with monthly active users of *Sberbank*'s online services numbering at 2.7 million. The market share of corporate loans is 32% (Sberbank 2023).

5 Methodology

This study suggests a modification of Ramamurti's framework of the evolution as an MNE and its application to examining the internationalisation strategies of emerging market financial MNEs. The revised model is presented in Table 2. The following indicators (criteria) are suggested for evaluating the stage of development as a financial MNE.

First, the depth of internationalisation is defined as the degree to which a financial MNE engages in foreign operations. In contrast to non-financial MNEs, financial MNEs do not conduct export activities; thus, the scope of their involvement in foreign markets can be measured simply by the share of foreign assets in total assets. Alternatively, UNCTAD's Transnationality Index or Transnational Activities Spread

Table 2 Stages of evolution as a financial MNE

Indicator of internationalisation/ stage of evolution	Stage 1. Infant financial MNE	Stage 2. Adolescent financial MNE	Stage 3. Mature financial MNE
Depth of internationalisation measured by ratio of foreign assets or Transnationality Index (TNI) or Transnational Activities Spread Index (TASI) (Ietto-Gillies 1997)	Ratio of foreign assets to total assets less than 10% TNI and TASI low	Ratio of foreign assets to total assets 11–25% TNI and TASI medium	Ratio of foreign assets to total assets more than 25% TNI and TASI high level
Breadth of internationalisation (geographical footprint, number of regions)	Few countries in home region; financial EMNEs is pursuing low-cost strategy; low diversification of foreign assets	Several countries in with the emphasis on home region; medium diversification of foreign assets	Dozens of countries in all major regions; high diversification of foreign assets
Importance of home-country-specific advantages (CSAs)	High	High to medium and falling	Medium to low and falling
Importance of home country government-created advantages (GCAs)	High	High to medium and falling	Medium to low and falling
Importance of firm-specific advantages (FSAs): – Asset-type FSAs (tangible and intangible assets) – Transaction-type FSAs	Low; brand is strong at home, unknown abroad Low	Low to medium, strong at home, up-and-coming abroad Low to medium	Medium to high; strong global brand Medium to high

Source Made by author with modifications of Ramamurti (2009, p. 420)

Index (TASI) (Ietto-Gillies 1997) can be applied. However, these indicators should be treated with caution, as the amount of foreign assets of financial MNEs is subject to strict financial regulation in many countries. In addition, financial MNEs often rely on their domestic customer base which must be significant in terms of generated assets and liabilities. Therefore, only large banks capable of paying the high entry costs to enter the financial markets of host countries have the opportunity to internationalise. Moreover, with the spread of digital banking and cryptocurrencies, assessing the exact amount of foreign assets has become a challenge.

Second, the breadth of internationalisation can be measured by the number of regions in which a financial MNE conducts its activities in the form of branches and subsidiaries. Representative offices of financial MNEs do not conduct financial activities and thus should be treated with caution, even though they represent the initial stage of the entry modes of financial MNEs. Alternatively, the Network Spread Index can be considered for application; however, as in the case of the depth of internationalisation, the development of digital banking and digital payments leaves leeway for financial MNEs to not be physically present in the host country, at least hypothetically.

Third, the importance of home CSAs (national factor endowments, comparative advantages of a home country) tends to be strong at the initial stages of the evolution of a financial MNE but tends to lose its importance afterwards. As mentioned by Ramamurti (2020), not all MNEs in a country have equal access to these CSAs; thus, more diligent consideration is needed in their assessment.

Fourth, GCAs are part of CSAs, but the focus in this case is on specific policies and government actions that allow financial MNEs to use them as competitive advantages in their internationalisation strategies.

Finally, FSAs are important for both asset and transaction types. Conventionally, the IB theory on emerging market MNEs argues that emerging market multinationals have weak FSAs and rely strongly on CSAs and GCAs at the initial stages of their evolution as MNEs. However, many emerging MNEs have proven to have strong transaction-type FSAs, the so-called advantages of common governance in terms of how to operate efficiently, both domestically and abroad. These may include the ability to organise intra-firm activities and manage large organisations, knowledge of institutions and relational capabilities, linkages and business networks, knowledge concerning where to buy and sell, and attracting cheap resources.

The suggested revised framework is applied to the case of *Sberbank* to evaluate its stage of evolution as a financial MNE at the peak of its foreign expansion in 2013.

6 Sberbank: The Stage of Evolution as an MNE

The share of foreign assets of *Sberbank* at the peak of its internationalisation in 2013 amounted to 12%. International corporate businesses mostly comprised *Denizbank* (Turkey), *Sberbank (Europe),* and the CIS (Ukraine, Belorussia, Kazakhstan), accounting for 46%, 27%, and 28% in December 2013, respectively. The share of international retail businesses in *Denizbank* (Turkey) was 79%; *Sberbank (Europe),* 16%; and in the CIS region, 5% (Sberbank 2013). In 2021, Sberbank had 288,000 employees in Russia and approximately 10% of all its workers were foreign employees, but not all were engaged in financial and banking businesses. Thus, we can conclude that the depth of internationalisation of *Sberbank* surpassed the 10% threshold only slightly.

By 2021, *Sberbank* had subsidiaries, branches, and representative offices across 22 countries. However, as mentioned previously, *Sberbank*'s geographical footprint is mostly in the home region (Europe, CIS), and thus it has low diversification of foreign assets across other continents; consequently, we can conclude that the breadth of its internationalisation remains low.

The reliance of *Sberbank* on home country CSAs is presumably high. The bank inherited the largest number of depositors and remains its monopolistic power in the Russian banking market. The volume of assets, liabilities, and net profits of *Sberbank* are significantly larger than those of the other banks. For instance, the net profits of *Sberbank* in 2021 were five times higher than those of *VTB* (2nd place) and nine times higher than *Alfa-Bank* (3rd place). A monopolistic position and a large number of domestic clients (75% of the total Russian population in 2022) provide opportunities for asset accumulation that can be utilised for internationalisation. As mentioned earlier, the financial and banking industries are highly regulated, and only large banks are capable of overcoming high foreign entry costs.

The role of the government in *Sberbank*'s internationalisation is disputable. While it is true that the Russian government remains the largest shareholder of *Sberbank* via the National Welfare Fund (Russia's sovereign wealth fund holds a 50 + 1% share), approximately half of its shares are traded on the stock exchange. In fact, in 2020, 43.5% of shares belonged to foreign investors, proving that it is a public company which strictly complies with global financial regulations and the standards of auditing and accounting. In addition, the shares of *Sberbank* remain the most popular on Russia's stock exchange. Russia's government does not actively support the internationalisation of *Sberbank*, as there are no official government programmes aimed at providing subsidies or preferences for companies pursuing internationalisation. Thus, the commercial interests of *Sberbank* both domestically and abroad prevail over the political agendas normally associated with state-owned banks. Previous research also confirms that Russia's banking sector is one in which the government has a high interest but a medium level of control. The government understands the self-sufficiency of Russian banks that have opportunities to invest abroad and does not directly control such operations (Panibratov 2016). Nevertheless, in pursuing the stability of the financial system in the domestic market, the government sometimes creates favourable conditions for state-owned banks that lead to further nationalisation and monopolisation of Russia's banking sector (Gorshkov 2020), thus indirectly creating the advantages of economies of scale for banks pursuing internationalisation.

Sberbank's brand name and digital ecosystem are its major sources of competitive advantage. In 2013, *Sberbank* ranked 61st in the Global 500 brand ranking and 13th in the Banking 500 ranking. *Brand Finance* calculated the brand value of *Sber*'s brand 17 times between 2007 and 2023: It was featured in 43 brand rankings, including the strongest and most valuable Russian brand, the biggest global brand, and the best banking brand. Since 2014, after the first round of sanctions, *Sberbank* searched for opportunities for domestic growth, and by accurately grasping changes in the global banking industry towards digitisation, it has started the shift to an active adoption of digital technologies. In 2020, *Sberbank* launched a rebranding campaign (*Sber* as a technological company) and announced the construction of its original digital ecosystem. The bank could successfully develop innovations in partnerships with Western (mostly US) companies. According to the *World Intellectual Property Organisation (WIPO)*, it was the top patent applicant in 2020 among all Russian companies, having filed a total of 30 patent applications. *Sber* was nominated as the best digital consumer bank, the bank with the best mobile banking adaptive site, the bank with the best open banking APIs, the best information security and fraud management, and the best in social media marketing and services in Central and Eastern Europe by the World's Best Digital Banks ranking 2021, evaluated by

Table 3 The evolution of Sberbank as a financial MNE

Indicator	Level	Stage as a financial MNE
Depth of internationalisation	Medium	Adolescent
Breath of internationalisation	Medium (regional MNE)	Adolescent
Importance of home CSAs	High	Infant
Importance of home country GSAs	Medium	Adolescent
Bank-specific advantages	Medium to high (regional rather than global brand)	Adolescent

Source Compiled by author

Global Finance. Thus, we can conclude that *Sberbank* has a medium-to-high level of bank-specific advantages.

A summary of our analysis based on Ramamurti's revised framework is provided in Table 3.

7 Economic Sanctions and Further Prospects of Internationalisation of Russian Financial MNEs

Under the stricter sanctions imposed since February 2022, many Russian banks have been forced to revisit their internationalisation strategies. China, India, and the UAE are now often considered major destinations for the establishment of new affiliates, as many Russian firms have accumulated the national currencies in these countries owing to the intensification of bilateral trade and economic relations in 2022–2024. In contrast to the internationalisation strategies in 1991–1999 and 2000–2022, branches are selected as a more favourable and less risky entry mode for foreign expansion, even though their establishment requires significantly larger entry costs than representative offices and subsidiaries.

The branches of *VTB* and *Sberbank* in India and China are utilised in international payments between Russian clients and their partners in those respective countries, with a focus on settlements in national currencies. For instance, as of July 2023, *Sberbank* reported that its branch in New Delhi had expanded significantly, with its capital reaching 4.9 billion rupees (approximately 65 million USD)—an increase by 1.8 times since the first quarter of 2022. *Alfa-bank* plans to launch both corporate and retail accounts and provide services such as international payments, currency exchange, factoring, and deposits in yuan in its planned Chinese branch (Uvarchev 2023).

However, the pivot to friendly jurisdictions is associated with several problems. First, the financial burden of opening branches is higher than that of subsidiaries. For instance, to open a branch in China, a foreign bank must have more than USD 20 billion in assets, while the minimum capital requirement in India is USD 25 million and USD 100 million in the UAE.

Second, foreign banks are required to submit an extensive list of documents, including information on the organisational structure of the parent bank, its shareholders, affiliated entities, and ultimate beneficiaries; market research analysis of a branch; business development plan; cash flow forecast for at least 3 years; and information on the banking system of the home country. Additional conditions, such as sound profits, goodwill and reputation, international experience, and solid rules and regulations on money laundering, must be fulfilled to gain access to the Chinese market. Overall, it takes approximately 2 years, on average, to satisfy all the conditions for establishing a branch. In India, there are strict restrictions on currency cross-border transactions; residents are prohibited from establishing foreign accounts and receiving loans from foreign institutions, except for transport, insurance, and construction companies. Thus, many Russian companies operating in India have excessive holdings in rupees due to such restrictions (Uvarchev 2023). Moreover, the establishment of branches in China and India is driven by the necessity of investing in and managing accumulated national currencies.

Third, the possibility of secondary sanctions against Chinese and Indian banks increased after the issuance of Executive Order 14,114 by US President Joseph Biden in December 2023. This executive order authorised the imposition of US sanctions on foreign financial institutions that either facilitate significant transitions on behalf of persons designated for operating in certain key sectors of the Russian economy, or provide services involving Russia's military-industrial complex. In January 2024, the three largest Chinese banks—the Industrial and Commercial Bank of China, China Construction Bank, and Bank of China—announced that they would halt operations with Russian banks under sanctions (Mingazov 2024). A few Turkish and UAE banks have also announced that they will impose restrictions on their transactions with Russian businesses.

Economic sanctions have inspired Russian banks to substitute foreign software with Russian analogues. On 30 March 2022, President Vladimir Putin signed a decree on cybersecurity at key financial institutions which restricted the purchase of foreign software and hardware systems from 31 March 2022 and completely prohibited the use of foreign software and hardware from 1 January 2025. Consequently, *Sberbank* has been trying to find solutions for the replacement of 85% of its software and hardware vendors and has had some success in implementing this import substitution policy. Many other larger banks, however, have requested that the Bank of Russia postpone this decision until 2027 (Mingazov 2023).

Thus, owing to the aforementioned hurdles, the establishment of branches in friendly jurisdictions is associated with significant risks. Currently, the establishment of a new functional system for cross-border payments remains a priority for many Russian banks, even though their physical presence in friendly jurisdictions is uncertain.

8 Conclusion

In this chapter, we modified the existing framework of the evolution as a financial MNE proposed by Ramamurti (2009, 2016, 2020) and applied it to the case of the largest Russian state-owned bank, *Sberbank*, which has actively pursued internationalisation since 2011. *Sberbank* has benefited significantly from globalisation and Russia's integration into the world economy, evolving from an inefficient state-owned bank established at the commencement of Russia's market transition to Russia's leading state-owned multinational bank.

We concluded that even at the peak of its internationalisation in 2013, *Sberbank* remained predominantly a regional financial MNE, as measured by the depth and breadth of its internationalisation. This is despite its possession of medium-to-high levels of bank-specific advantages in Central and Eastern Europe. Thus, with some limitations in assessment methodology, *Sberbank* is a representative case of an adolescent financial MNE. Its strong brand name in the region and successful utilisation of digital and online technologies have laid a solid foundation for its further evolution as a financial MNE.

However, under the economic and financial sanctions imposed since the 24th of February 2022, major Russian banks physically withdrew from European and a few CIS markets, and halted correspondent operations with foreign banks located in these regions. Many Russian banks reduced their holdings in US dollars, euros, and yens; transformed their assets and liability structure; and pursued new sources of funding and destinations for their foreign expansion. The feasibility of pivoting to friendly jurisdictions, however, remains uncertain because of the significant financial and administrative burdens and restrictions, as well as the increased risk of secondary sanctions.

Sberbank's expansion into the European market lasted for less than a decade; thus, it can be posited that the impact of the sanctions has been considerable. Nevertheless, *Sberbank* recorded relatively high profits in 2023, proving its resilience against the sanctions and strength in the domestic market. However, the prospects of reorientation towards new foreign markets in friendly jurisdictions, such as China, India, and the UAE, remain unclear.

Acknowledgements This research was supported by following research funds: (1) JSPS KAKENHI Fund for the Promotion of Joint International Research (Fostering Joint International Research (B), 22KK0023 entitled *International joint research for the construction of emerging MNC theory and the analysis of changes in the international division of labour*; (2) grant-in-aid of the project-based collaborative research entitled *Comparative research on Slavic-Eurasian and Asian multinationals and the structural changes in the international division of labour* provided by the Slavic-Eurasian Research Centre, Hokkaido University, Japan; and (3) Joint usage (individual research projects) grant for the AY 2023 on the comprehensive research focussed on the Slavic-Eurasian region (former Soviet Union and Eastern Europe) entitled *The Impact of Economic Sanctions on Russian Banks' Foreign Expansion* provided by the Slavic-Eurasian Research Centre, Hokkaido University, Japan.

The author is indebted to Professor Emeritus Ravi Ramamurti (Northeastern University) and Professor Emeritus Shinichiro Tabata (Hokkaido University) for their useful suggestions and constructive feedback on the earlier drafts of this research.

References

Abalkina A (2010) Vzaimnoe uchastie bankov v regione SNG: Masshtabi i tendencii (Mutual participation of banks in CIS region: Scale and recent trends). Bankovskoe Delo 2:29–34 (in Russian)

Abalkina AA (2014) Formy i methody ekspansii rossijskih bankov za rubezh (Forms and methods of Russian banks' foreign expansion). Dengi i Kredit 3:22–26 (in Russian)

Abalkina A, Ivanova K (2014) Rossiyskie banki v stranakh dal'nego zarubezh'ya (Expansion of Russian Banks outside Commonwealth of Independent States). World Economy and International Relations 5:21–30 (in Russian). https://doi.org/10.20542/0131-2227-2014-5-21-30 (in Russian)

Batyrov T (2023) VTB podal isk na 113 millionov evro k svoej byvshej evropejskoj "dochke" (VTB has filed a case worth 113 million euro against its former subsidiary in Europe). https://www.forbes.ru/finansy/496638-vtb-podal-isk-na-113-mln-k-svoej-byvsej-evropejskoj-docke (in Russian). Accessed 29 Apr 2024

Collinson S, Narula R, Rugman AM (2020) International business. Pearson, London

Gorshkov V (2013) Foreign banking in Russia: an analysis of inward-outward expansion. J Compar Econ Stud 8:77–107

Gorshkov V (2020) State-permeated banking sector: recent trends in Russia's banking. Compar Econ Rev 27(2):1–27

Ietto-Gillies G (1997) What do internationalization indices measure? CIBS Research Papers in International Business London South Bank University CIBS, pp 6–97

Ietto-Gillies G (2022) Transnationality in the XXI century. Concept and indicators. Crit Perspect Intern Bus 18(3):338–361. https://doi.org/10.1108/cpoib-11-2020-0135

Karasyuk E (2014) Sberbank: the rebirth of Russia's financial giant. Glagoslav Publications

Larioshina L (2019) Rezul'taty ekspansii rossiyskikh bankov za rubezh na primere DenizBank v Turtsii (The results of the expansion of Russian banks abroad on the example of Denizbank in Turkey). Vestnik Instituta Ekonomiki Rossijskoj Akademii Nauk 3:182–194 (in Russian)

Luo Y, Tung LR (2007) International expansion of emerging market enterprises: a springboard perspective. J Intern Bus Stud 38:481–498. https://doi.org/10.1057/palgrave.jibs.8400275

Mathews JA (2017) Dragon multinationals powered by linkage, leverage and learning: a review and development. Asia Pacific J Manag 34:769–775

Mingazov S (2023) Krupnye banki poprosili otlozhit' perekhod na rossiyskiy sistemnyy soft (Large banks requested to postpone the transition to Russian software and hardware). Forbes. https://www.forbes.ru/finansy/496078-krupnye-banki-poprosili-otlozit-perehod-na-rossijskij-sistemnyj-soft (in Russian). Accessed 29 Apr 2024

Mingazov S (2024) Tri krupneyshikh banka KNR otkazalis' prinimat' platezhi ot bankov Rossii pod sanktsiyami (Three largest Chinese banks refused to accept payments from Russian banks under sanctions). Forbes. https://www.forbes.ru/finansy/506636-tri-krupnejsih-banka-knr-otkazalis-prinimat-platezi-ot-bankov-rossii-pod-sankciami (in Russian). Accessed 29 Apr 2024

Nikitina YNV, Volkova IO (2016) Strategii internatsionalizatsii rossiyskikh bankov i sposoby ikh vykhoda na zarubezhnye rynki (Internationalization strategies of Russian banks and their entry modes into foreign markets). Nauchnye Vedomosti. Econ Ser Inf 16(39):61–73 (in Russian)

Panibratov A (2013) Russian multinationals: from regional supremacy to global lead. Routledge, London

Panibratov A (2016) Home government influence on Russian MNEs: balancing control against interest. Intern J Emerg Mark 11(4):474–496. https://doi.org/10.1108/IJoEM-11-2014-0193

Panibratov A, Verba C (2011) Russian banking sector: key points of international expansion. Organ Mark Emerg Econ 2(1):63–74. https://doi.org/10.15388/omee.2011.2.1.14290

Panibratov A (2010) Russian multinationals: entry strategies and post-entry operations. Electronic publications of Pan-European Institute, Turku School of Economics 15. https://www.utu.fi/sites/default/files/media/Panibratov_netti_final.pdf. Accessed 29 Apr 2024

Ramamurti R (2009) What have we learned about emerging-market MNEs? In: Ramamurti R, Singh JV (eds) Emerging multinationals in emerging markets. Cambridge University Press, New York, pp 399–426

Ramamurti R (2016) Internationalization and innovation in emerging markets. Strat Manag J 37:74–83. https://doi.org/10.1002/smj.2553

Ramamurti R (2020) Analytical misunderstandings about emerging-market multinationals. J Compar Econ Stud 15:9–20

RBK News (2023) Sberbank vyshel s bankovskogo rynka Evropejskogo soyuza (Sberbank has withdrawn its business from the EU). https://www.rbc.ru/business/16/06/2023/648c4bcb9a79470a2dd5ba28 (in Russian). Accessed 29 Apr 2024

Sberbank (2023) Godovoy otchet 2022 [Annual report 2022]. https://www.sberbank.com/common/img/uploaded/_new_site/com/gosa2023/sber-ar-2022-ru.pdf (in Russian). Accessed 29 Apr 2024

Sberbank (2013) Strategiya razvitiya Sberbanka na period 2014–2018 (Sberbank's development strategy for 2014–2018). https://www.sberbank.com/common/img/uploaded/ir/docs/sberbankdevelopmentstrategyfor2014-2018_ru.pdf (in Russian). Accessed 29 Apr 2024

Teece DJ, Pisano G, Shuen A (1997) Dynamic capabilities and strategic management. Strat Manag J 18(7):509–533

Uvarchev L (2023) Na predstavitel'skie dokhody. Zachem rossiyskie banki rasshiryayut zarubezhnuyu filial'nuyu set' (For representative profits. Why are Russian bank expanding foreign affiliate network?). Kommersant. https://www.kommersant.ru/doc/6323329 (in Russian). Accessed 29 Apr 2024

Victor Gorshkov is an associate professor at the Faculty of International Economic Studies, University of Niigata Prefecture (Japan). He previously served as a Dean at the Faculty of International Liberal Arts, Kaichi International University (Japan). He received his M.A. in international economics and finance from Khabarovsk State University of Economics and Law (Russia) and Ph.D. in Economics from Kyoto University (Japan). He is a charter member of the Japanese Society for Comparative Economic Studies. Victor has taught part-time at Kanagawa University, Rikkyo University, and Keio University in Japan and conducted research as a visiting scholar at the Institute of Economic Research, Kyoto University and the Slavic-Eurasian Research Center, Hokkaido University. His research interests are in the field of international economics, comparative economic systems, international business and emerging market economies. Victor's recent publications include the following: Gorshkov, V. (2024). Chapter 10. The Peculiar Features of Emerging and Transition Economies. pp. 196–210. In R. Wakasugi (ed.). *International and Regional Economy: Learning from the Foundations*. Tokyo: Bunshido (in Japanese); Gorshkov, V. (2022). Cashless Payment in Emerging Markets: The Case of Russia. *Asia and the Global Economy*, 2, 100033; and Gorshkov, V. (2020). Chapter 4. Fundamentals and Recent Trends in Russian Banking. pp. 73–93. In S. Rosefielde (ed.). *Putin's Russia: Economy, Defence and Foreign Policy*. Singapore: World Scientific Publishers.

Conclusion: Evolution of Emerging Market Multinationals from Asia and Europe

Victor Gorshkov

Abstract The objectives of this chapter are twofold. First, by calculating the outward foreign direct investment performance index and examining the forward and backward participation of selected emerging economies from Asia and Europe in global supply chains, we demonstrate that there have been significant structural changes in the international division of labour owing to the enhancing role of emerging market multinationals in the global economy. Second, by utilising Ramamurti's framework of the stage of evolution as a multinational enterprise (MNE), we examine three case studies: Taiwan Semiconductor Manufacturing Company Limited (TSMC, Taiwan), Lenovo (China), and Sberbank (Russia), and provide evidence that these companies have shifted from an infant to adolescent and mature stages in their evolution. Finally, based on the results of our empirical analysis, we demonstrate the limitations of Ramamurti's framework and outline possible directions for its modification.

Keywords Emerging multinationals · Stage of evolution · Taiwan · China · Russia

1 Introduction

The phenomenon of emerging markets continues to be in the spotlight in both academia and business. In recent decades, their remarkable growth, increased volume of foreign direct investment (FDI) inflows and outflows, and shifting roles in the global economy are evident. For instance, the share of 23 emerging market economies, as defined by the Russell Index Global Guidebook Country Classifications, in global outward FDI flows increased from 3.5 to 25.9% and in global FDI stock from 4.6 to 16.2% from 1990 to 2022.

The increase in global FDI outflows from emerging market economies has raised interest in emerging market multinationals (MNEs) in international business (IB) research (Gorshkov 2018). Some studies have aimed to understand how firms from emerging markets become MNEs, how dependent they are on home country-specific

---

V. Gorshkov (✉)
Faculty of International Economic Studies, University of Niigata Prefecture, Niigata, Japan
e-mail: vgorshkov@unii.ac.jp

© The Author(s), under exclusive license to Springer Nature Singapore Pte Ltd. 2024
Y. Nakahara (ed.), *Emerging Multinationals from Asia and Europe*,
SpringerBriefs in Economics, https://doi.org/10.1007/978-981-97-4042-0_5

advantages (CSAs) and government-created advantages (GCAs), and what kind of firm-specific advantages (FSAs) they utilise in their internationalisation (Ramamurti 2009, 2016, 2020).

In this book, we addressed the issues of internationalisation of firms from emerging markets in Asia and Europe. In particular, we attempted to understand their stages of evolution as MNEs based on the framework suggested by Ramamurti (2009).

One medium-sized emerging market economy, Taiwan, and two large emerging economies, China and Russia, were selected for this research. The statistics for Poland, a medium-sized economy in Europe, has been included for comparative purposes.

Our key research questions were as follows: At the macro-level, by calculating the FDI performance index and examining the forward and backward participation of the selected emerging economies in global supply chains, we tried to understand whether there were any visible structural changes in the international division of labour owing to the enhancing role of emerging market MNEs in the global economy.

At the micro-level, we aimed to determine whether there was any evidence that a few emerging market MNEs evolved from the infant to adolescent or mature stages of development as MNEs, and whether they could successfully nurture their FSAs.

The remainder of this chapter provides a short overview of the research findings, outlines the limitations, and presents further research directions.

2 FDI Performance Index for Emerging Multinationals from Europe and Asia

The FDI performance index was developed by United Nations Conference on Trade and Development (UNCTAD) to measure a country's relative position worldwide in terms of inward or outward FDI (flow or stock) performance. That is, it captures a country's relative success in attracting and investing in global FDI. The FDI performance index is calculated as the ratio of a country's share of global FDI flows (or stocks) to its share of global gross domestic product (GDP) (Eq. 1). By considering the share of a countries' GDP in the world GDP, it represents a more realistic comparative picture of FDI performance among countries than indicators such as shares of inward or outward FDI in GDP.

$$FDI\ performance\ index = \frac{FDIi/FDIw}{GDPi/GDPw} * 100 \qquad (1)$$

If a country's share of global FDI matches its relative share of world GDP, the FDI performance index is equal to one.

The outward FDI performance index reflects (1) FSAs that firms exploit abroad or wish to augment through internationalisation and (2) home and host CSAs, such as relative market production or transportation costs, skills, supply chains, infrastructure, and technology support. For small economies, the index tends to be

Conclusion: Evolution of Emerging Market Multinationals from Asia … 73

higher, suggesting that these courtiers have highly competitive enterprises with FSAs, allowing them to compete in foreign markets. Additionally, it is an indicator that they have relatively small domestic markets sizes and are driven to expand abroad (UNCTAD 2004).

Figures 1 and 2 show data on inward and outward FDI performance indices for selected economies between 1995 and 2021.

For Taiwan, the outward FDI performance index exceeds one and is significantly higher than the inward FDI performance index, confirming the enhanced role of Taiwanese MNEs in global outward FDI. In particular, previous research has confirmed that Taiwanese MNEs, such as Foxconn and TSMC, have evolved to dominate both the capital- and labour-intensive segments of the global electronics production value chain, which is a unique situation as countries tend to dominate only one segment of the value chain (Hao and Bu 2022).

Taiwan is contrasted by another medium-sized country, Poland, for which the inward FDI performance index was high in 1995–2015 and has been declining recently. This suggests that Poland provides significant host CSAs (low labour cost,

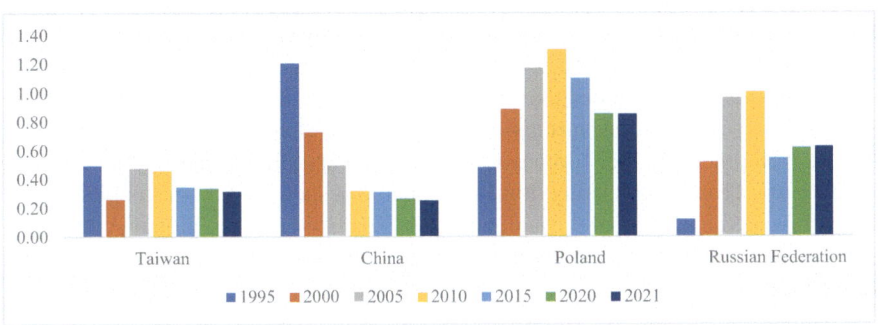

Fig. 1 Inward FDI performance index. *Source* Calculated by the author based on the UNCTAD statistics. *Note* FDI stock, GDP in current prices

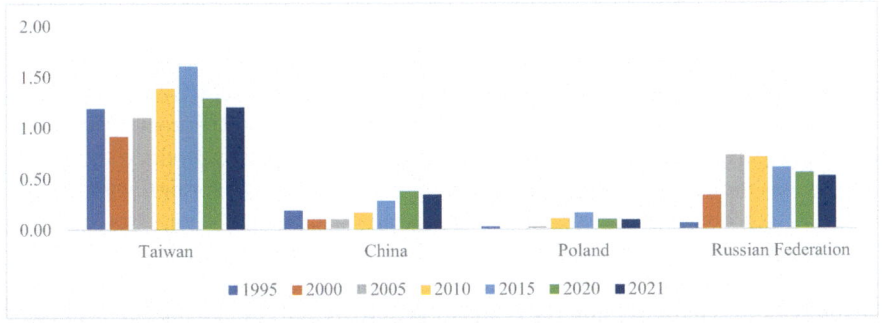

Fig. 2 Outward FDI performance index. *Source* Calculated by the author based on the UNCTAD statistics. *Note* FDI stock, GDP in current prices

agglomeration advantages for German automobile industries) for European and other developed countries' MNEs. The low FDI performance index suggests that Polish MNEs are not actively expanding into foreign markets.

For China, both indices are currently lower than one, suggesting that it has a very large domestic economy. The inward FDI performance index decreases in the respective periods, whereas the outward FDI performance index tends to increase. This suggests that the policy of inward FDI attraction, particularly into the special economic zones, such as Shenzen, Zhuhai, and Shantou located in the Guangdong Province established in the 1980s, has been effective in encouraging China's private sector to gradually develop its domestic manufacturing capacity (Lowe 2020). Outward FDI has been increasing because of the *Go Global Strategy*, first announced in 2000, which encourages Chinese enterprises to invest overseas.

The inward FDI performance index for Russia grew from 1995 to 2010 and exceeded one in 2010, suggesting that Russia's economy benefited from the inflow of FDI in relation to its economy size. However, the sectoral distribution of FDI was uneven in the natural resources, retail, and trade sectors, accumulating higher FDI spillover effects than in the manufacturing sector. The outward FDI performance index steadily grew from 1995 to 2010; however, further expansion overseas by Russian MNEs has slowed since 2014 owing to the deterioration of the geopolitical environment and the economic sanctions imposed on Russia.

Overall, it can be concluded that selective emerging market MNEs from Asia have been more successful in accumulating inward FDI and successfully transferring it to the development of their domestic production capabilities than their European counterparts. Over time, raising domestic capabilities allowed them to build export competitiveness and expand through outward FDI. However, the global context and timing under which emerging market MNEs from Asia and Europe internationalised was different.

3 Forward and Backward Participation of Emerging Market Multinationals from Asia and Europe

Examining a country's participation in global value chains (GVCs) is useful to understand whether there are any structural changes in the international division of labour owing to the rise of emerging market MNEs from Asia and Europe. Individual economies participate in GVCs by importing foreign input to produce the goods and services they export (backward participation, measured as foreign value-added content of exports) and exporting domestically produced inputs to partners in charge of downstream production stages (forward participation, measured as domestic value-added sent to third economies). Forward participation measures the technological capability of a country because the production of parts and components to be utilised in the supply chain of other countries requires high quality.

Figure 3 shows the dynamics of the value-added components of gross exports in 2010 and 2018. In Taiwan, forward participation increased from 18.7 to 20.9%. However, the total breakdown of value-added components shows that Taiwan is much more dependent on the foreign value-added content of exports, which is significantly higher than that of China. Backward participation in Taiwan's top export industries was approximately 36–41% (Table 1). In the case of computers and electronic products, previous research has shown that Taiwan plays a pivotal role in the entire global consumer electronics supply chain, leading to a capital-intensive segment (Taiwan Semiconductor Manufacturing Company, *TSMC*), such as the production of semiconductor chips and other electronic components, and a labour-intensive segment (*Foxconn*), such as the final assembly of personal computers and smartphones (Hao and Bu 2022). Taiwan managed to overcome its limitation of having a small-sized domestic economy by integrating into the world market through export-oriented industrialisation and specialising in the official equipment manufacturing (OEM) and official design manufacturing (ODM) manufacturing (Nakahara 2020). Taiwan's overall net gains from GVC participation are shown in Fig. 4, suggesting that its economy is still highly dependent on labour-intensive segments; however, there is an increase in capital-intensive segments as well.

In China, the domestic value added to third economies (forward participation) increased from 17.5 to 19.3%, while the foreign value-added content of exports (backward participation) declined during this period. This result is consistent with previous studies (Kobayashi 2021) and suggests that Chinese firms have been successful in producing domestic value-added and supplying parts and components that are utilised in GVCs. This indicates the improvement of the technological and production capabilities of Chinese firms engaged in international trade. The top export industries in

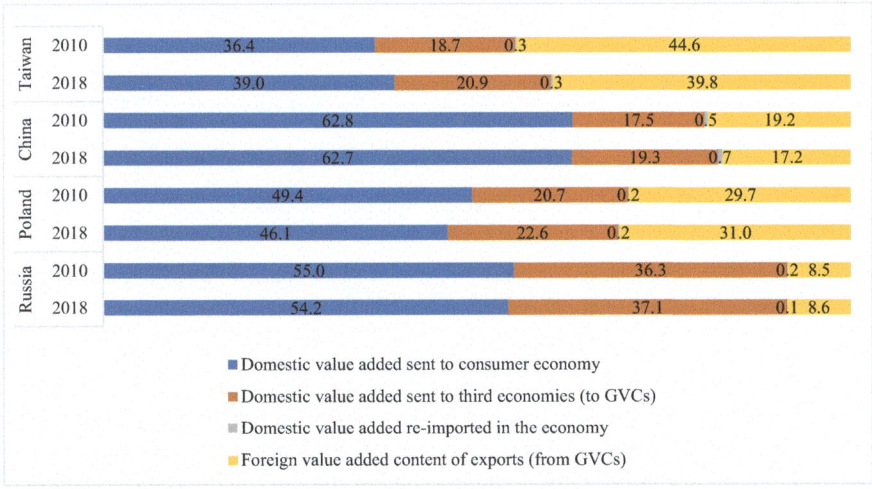

Fig. 3 Value-added components of gross exports, 2010 and 2018. *Source* Compiled by the author based on the WTO calculations on the OECD TiVA database

Table 1 Top export industries—domestic and foreign value added of exports in 2018 (as a percentage share in industry total gross exports)

Taiwan's top export industries	Domestic value	Foreign value	China's top export industries	Domestic value	Foreign value
Computer/electronic products	59	41	Computer/electronic products	72.9	27.1
Chemical products	62.1	37.9	Textiles and clothing	87	13
Wholesale and retail trade	63.2	36.8	Electrical equipment	81.2	18.8
Poland's top export industries	Domestic value	Foreign value	Russia's top export industries	Domestic value	Foreign value
Wholesale and retail trade	85.8	14.2	Mining (energy products)	96.2	3.8
Motor vehicles	51.2	48.8	Petroleum products	94.2	5.8
Land transport	75.8	24.2	Wholesale and retail trade	93.4	6.6

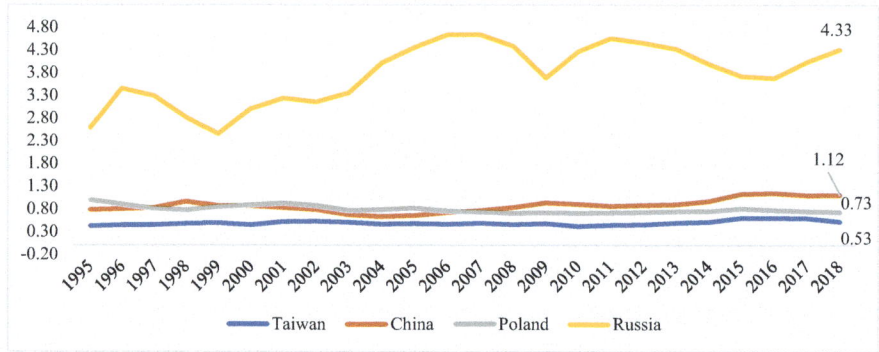

Fig. 4 Ratio of forward-to-backward participation (net value gains from GVC participation). *Source* Calculated by the author based on the OECD TiVA database

China in 2018 were computer and electronic products, textiles and clothing, and electrical equipment; domestic value-added in these industries significantly surpassed foreign value-added (Table 1). Overall, gains from GVC participation in China, calculated as the ratio of forward participation to backward participation, have exceeded one since 2014, suggesting that China has been gradually overcoming its role as a provider of simple assembly activities in product manufacturing (Fig. 4).

Poland's forward participation has increased from 20.7 to 22.6% from 2010 to 2018 (Fig. 3). The share of domestic value-added in Poland's top export industries, such as motor vehicles and land transport, is relatively high (Table 1); however, as in the case of Taiwan, foreign value-added accounts for approximately one-third of the value-added components of gross exports. The total net benefits from GVC participation are below one, suggesting that the country must further upgrade its production capabilities to generate higher net benefits from GVC participation.

Russia's forward participation is the highest among the selected economies (Fig. 3); however, it is mostly generated in the primary (mining and petroleum products) and tertiary (wholesale and retail) sectors. The manufacturing sector (automobile and civil aviation) depends largely on the supply of foreign parts and components. Therefore, Russia participates in GVCs as a provider of natural resources that other economies use in their final demand and exports to third countries (Volgina 2018). Thus, its net gains from GVC participation are significantly higher than those of other countries (Fig. 4), and it is deeply integrated into the global economy. The low level of GVC participation in the manufacturing sector explains why only Russia's natural resource and financial sector MNEs are present in the global MNEs' rankings.

4 Stage of Evolution as an MNE for Emerging Market Multinationals from Asia and Europe

Previous studies have confirmed that research on the internationalisation of emerging market MNEs remains in the initial phase of development, mainly because of the lack of synthetic theoretical foundations, discrepancies in methodology, and the fragmented research results. A key theoretical debate to date is whether developed country MNEs are similar or different from emerging market MNEs, whether we need new theories to explain internationalisation patterns of emerging MNEs or the existing IB theories can be extended to understand internationalisation strategies of emerging MNEs (Bıçakcıoğlu-Peynirci 2023).

Ramamurti (2009, 2016, 2020) highlights the importance of research on emerging markets to strengthen existing IB theories, advocating the necessity of considering the stage of evolution as an MNE when comparing emerging market MNEs with incumbent developed market MNEs. In this book, we utilised his stage-of-evolution framework to examine cases of emerging MNEs from Asia and Europe.

Three case studies, namely, *TSMC* (Taiwan), *Lenovo* (China), and *Sberbank* (Russia), were selected to examine their stages of evolution as MNEs. *TSMC* and *Lenovo* are representatives of the computer and electronics industries, in which Taiwan and China have significantly improved their competitive advantages. *Sberbank* was selected as it provides one of the most successful cases of internationalisation, apart from natural resource sector MNEs. Overall, with some limitations in the methodology, we conclude that these three cases can be regarded as examples of emerging market MNEs that have been gradually shifting from the infant to adolescent and mature stages in their evolution.

Chapter 2 highlighted that *TSMC* has several competitive advantages, such as technological capability, capital and financial resources, involvement in both the production and design of chips, a significant amount of R&D, and dedication to customers as a manufacturing service company, which makes it a leading player in the global semiconductor industry. Recently, *TSMC* has accelerated its so-called 'pushed internationalisation' being enticed by foreign governments to locate its manufacturing bases in the United States, Germany, and Japan owing to geopolitical tensions that may lead to US–China economic decoupling. *TSMC* is one of two firms, worldwide, capable of producing five nanometre chips, the other being Samsung.

Government-created specific advantages (GSAs) play a significant role in the evolution of *TSMC*. The Taiwanese government assured the company's technological leadership through deliberate planning and indicative government policies, such as the establishment of the Industrial Technology Research Institute, a public institution funded by the government, and the Hsinchu Science Park, a high-tech cluster located in proximity to Taiwan's best universities. In addition, the government stimulated the return of Taiwanese scientists and engineers from the United States, who were motivated by the growing possibilities at home. The newly established ecosystem attracted many semiconductor design firms (fabless firms) to the Hsinchu Science Park, thus providing growth opportunities for semiconductor fabs such as *TSMC*. Continuous R&D of over 8% of its annual revenue has been achieved through its unrivalled size and economies of scale (Hao and Bu 2022). Despite its low levels of depth and breadth of internationalisation, *TSMC* remains the most prominent firm in the global semiconductor industry. In summary, Chapter 2 provided evidence that *TSMC* could successfully nurture its FSAs and had moved to a more mature stages of development as an MNE.

Chapter 3 analysed the case of *Lenovo* and concluded that it can be classified as an adolescent MNE. The dependence on home CSAs for *Lenovo* remains relatively high; however, the company has a world-famous strong brand awareness and currently accounts for 23% of the world shares in PC production. In addition, *Lenovo* has been rapidly increasing its geographical footprint by establishing R&D centres in the United States and Europe. Previous research also confirms that Lenovo has successfully nurtured its FSAs as a technology innovator which utilises the patented technology and talents of Chinese returnees as its core competencies. The company focussed on acquiring overseas talent and partnering with well-known brands (such as IBM PC business) to expand its distribution channels and capitalise on brand equity to launch new product lines, such as the Lenovo Yoga, Lenovo Z series, and Lenovo-IBM ThinkPad (Su et al. 2022).

In Chap. 4, we demonstrated that Russia's *Sberbank* possessed medium-to high-level bank-specific advantages in Central and Eastern Europe; however, even at its internationalisation peak in 2013, it remained predominantly a regional financial MNE, as measured by the depth and breadth of its internationalisation. Nevertheless, its strong brand name in the region and successful utilisation of digital and online technologies have laid solid grounds for its further evolution as a financial MNE. The monopolistic advantages of *Sberbank* in the home market account for its ability to compete globally, a feature typical of many Russian MNEs (Grätz 2014). In addition, for Russian banks in Central and Eastern Europe, asset-based FSAs are closely connected to transaction-based FSAs (Weiner 2020). The banking sector in Russia remains of high interest to the government but is not excessively controlled, especially when it comes to internationalisation. Consequently, we concluded that *Sberbank* had gradually evolved into the adolescent stage as a financial MNE; however, its further internationalisation was halted owing to economic and financial sanctions imposed on Russian banks because of the geopolitical and military conflict with Ukraine.

The selected case studies examined in this book provide only partial evidence of the evolution of emerging market MNEs from Asia and Europe to more mature stages of development. However, they enrich our understanding of the internationalisation strategies of emerging market MNEs, the differences in FSAs between developed and emerging market MNEs, the importance of analysing host and home CSAs and GSAs, and the global context of a firm's internationalisation.

5 Towards a New Theory of Evolution as an MNE

From the empirical analysis of the case studies presented in this book, we outline a few points that need to be addressed for the further development of Ramamurti's framework of evolution as an MNE (Ramamurti 2009, 2016, 2020).

First, within this framework, home CSAs and GCAs should be considered separately. As mentioned in Chap. 3, in China, the government exercises great influence over both state- and private-owned enterprises; thus, it seems arguable to assume that over time, GSAs will diminish, especially considering the fact that previous research has indicated that China represents a case of state-permeated capitalism, categorised by dense informal relationships between public authorities and large domestic corporations, in which the government provides various forms of domestic state support to Chinese private MNEs (Nolke 2014). In addition, the Chinese government has recently been concerned about capital outflows and has thus put stricter restrictions on the cross-border movement of capital. Hence, there is a possibility that government policies may in fact turn into a disadvantage for Chinese MNEs.

Second, in large emerging economies, domestic market size is a crucial source of CSAs. State-permeated economies, such as China, Brazil, and India, benefit significantly from their large domestic markets, which allow domestic firms to pursue internationalisation and enjoy significant economies of scale and cost advantages (Nolke 2014, 2023), which often serve as sources of their competitive advantages and transaction-type FSAs. For instance, in this book, we show that both *Lenovo* and *Sberbank* utilise their domestic markets to generate financial strength, access technological capabilities, and a large consumer base.

Third, the notion that FDI tends to increase and eventually surpass exports when MNEs move to the mature stage of development is disputable. For instance, in the labour-intensive segments of the ICT sector, most products are predominantly produced in low-wage Asian countries and then exported to consumer economies; therefore, it is hard to imagine that this structure will change as countries like China still enjoy large economies of scale in their domestic markets. Even in the case of *TSMC*, the expansion to the United States and Japan represents the case of the so-called 'pushed internationalisation' owing to the geopolitical tensions and the U.S.–China rivalry. In the short- to medium-term, it is highly unlikely to reach scale effects similar to what *TSMC* is currently relishing in the domestic market.

Finally, the existing framework should be modified to incorporate broader research into the evolution of digital and financial MNEs. Recent studies have demonstrated that our conceptualisation of MNEs, based on FDI and the measurement of breadth and depth of internationalisation, needs to be reconsidered owing to enhanced digitalisation and financialisaton of the world economy, growth in externalisation of business activities, and the related rise in non-equity modes of internationalisation, such as outsourcing, OEM, and ODM. For instance, digital MNEs utilise business models, in which users are not necessarily generate primary sources of revenues for the company, and which tend to maintain large cash holdings, and tend to have non-location-bound production processes and services. Thus, digital MNEs have lower levels of foreign investment and assets than total and foreign sales and revenues (Ietto-Gillies 2022) and are sometimes described as asset-light business models (Trentini et al. 2022). Our case studies of *TSMC* and *Lenovo* confirm that these two companies, while operating globally and generating the majority of their sales and revenues abroad, have relatively small amounts of overseas assets. As digital MNEs and global firms in the ICT sector are rapidly emerging in China and other emerging markets (Gorshkov and Podoba 2022), further investigation of the internationalisation strategies of these MNEs remains a crucial task.

The same applies to financial MNEs, for which the breadth of internationalisation, measured by the number of foreign affiliates, seems to have a low connection with the volume of foreign assets, particularly fixed assets (Ietto-Gillies 2022). In addition, the digitalisation of financial services allows banks to conduct operations without a physical presence in the host country, as demonstrated in the example of online banking for *Sberbank* in Germany. Emerging markets are pioneering in the introduction of digital technologies, such as digital payments (Gorshkov 2022). Hence, the scope of emerging financial MNEs' activities might be underestimated.

Overall, further research will have to look deeper into the aspects mentioned above and other untapped issues of the evolution of emerging market MNEs to better grasp the features and patterns of their internationalisation and enrich the existing IB theory.

Acknowledgements This research was supported by the JSPS KAKENHI Fund for the Promotion of Joint International Research (Fostering Joint International Research (B), 22KK0023 entitled *International joint research for the construction of emerging MNC theory and the analysis of changes in the international division of labour*, grant-in-aid of the project-based collaborative research for the AY 2022 entitled *Comparative research on Slavic-Eurasian and Asian multinationals and the structural changes in the international division of labour* provided by the Slavic-Eurasian Research Centre, Hokkaido University, Japan.

References

Bıçakcıoğlu-Peynirci N (2023) Internationalization of emerging market multinational enterprises: a systematic literature review and future directions. J Bus Res 114002. https://doi.org/10.1016/j.jbusres.2023.114002

Gorshkov V (2018) Emerging multinationals: some theoretical and empirical considerations. J Compar Econ Stud 13:7–12

Gorshkov V (2022) Cashless payment in emerging markets: the case of Russia. Asia Glob Econ 2(1):100033. https://doi.org/10.1016/j.aglobe.2022.100033

Gorshkov V, Podoba Z (2022) Internationalization of multinational enterprises from North-East Asia. In: Haba K, Canavero A, Mizobata S (eds) 100 years of world wars and post-war regional collaboration. How to create 'new world order'. Springer, Singapore, pp 265–280. https://doi.org/10.1007/978-981-16-9970-2_21

Grätz J (2014) Russia's multinationals: network state capitalism goes global. In: Nolke A (ed) Multinational corporations from emerging markets. State capitalism 3.0. Palgrave Macmillan, London, pp 90–108. https://doi.org/10.1057/9781137359506_6

Hao D, Bu N (2022) The broad and pivotal roles of Taiwanese electronics industry in the global electronics supply chain: a case study of Foxconn and TSMC. In: Wu T, Bu N (eds) International business in the New Asia-Pacific. Advances in theory and practice of emerging markets. Springer, pp 161–196. https://doi.org/10.1007/978-3-030-87621-0_6

Ietto-Gillies G (2022) Transnationality in the XXI century. Concept and indicators. Crit Perspect Intern Bus 18(3):338–361. https://doi.org/10.1108/cpoib-11-2020-0135

Kobayashi T (2021) Chyugoku seizogyo no kokusaikyousouryoku. Boeki to genchi chyotasuritsu no deta wo mochita bunseki (International competitiveness of Chinese manufacturing industry. An analysis of foreign trade and local procurement rates). Matsuyama Daigaku Ronshyu (Bull Matusyama Univ) 33(5):129–153 (in Japanese)

Lowe P (2020) Transnational and multinational corporations in the global economy. Independently published

Nakahara Y (2020) Structural change in Taiwanese manufacturing foreign direct investment in the 21st century. J Compar Econ Stud 15:21–44

Nolke A (2014) Private Chinese multinationals and the long shadow of the state. In: Nolke A (ed) Multinational corporations from emerging markets. State capitalism 3.0. Palgrave Macmillan, London, pp 75–89. https://doi.org/10.1057/9781137359506_5

Nolke A (2023) Foreign direct investment. In: Nolke A (ed) Second image IPE. Palgrave Macmillan, London, pp 175–202. https://doi.org/10.1007/978-3-031-37693-1_7

Ramamurti R (2009) What have we learned about emerging-market MNEs? In: Ramamurti R, Singh JV (eds) Emerging multinationals in emerging markets. Cambridge University Press, New York, pp 399–426

Ramamurti R (2016) Internationalization and innovation in emerging markets. Strat Manag J 37:74–83. https://doi.org/10.1002/smj.2553

Ramamurti R (2020) Analytical misunderstandings about emerging-market multinationals. J Compar Econ Stud 15:9–20

Su M, Shi H, Zhao M, Tan K (2022) Emerging dragons: how do Chinese companies expand overseas? In: Wu T, Bu N (eds) International business in the new Asia-Pacific. Advances in theory and practice of emerging markets. Springer, pp 213–238. https://doi.org/10.1007/978-3-030-87621-0_8

Trentini C, de Camargo Mainente J, Santos-Paulino AU (2022) The evolution of digital MNEs: an empirical note. Transnatl Corp J 29(1):163–187. Available at SSRN: https://ssrn.com/abstract=4096759. Accessed 29 Apr 2024

UNCTAD (2004) Small countries invest relatively more abroad than big ones: UNCTAD releases new outward FDI performance index. https://press.un.org/en/2004/tad1996.doc.htm. Accessed 29 Apr 2024

Volgina N (2018) Russia in global value chains: levels of participation and distribution of gains. In: Sergi BS (ed) Exploring the future of Russia's economy and markets. Emerald Publishing, Towards sustainable economic development, pp 217–234

Weiner C (2020) Russian multinational direct investment in East Central European countries. In: Szunomár Á (ed) Emerging-market multinational enterprises in East Central Europe. Palgrave Macmillan, London, pp 153–195. https://doi.org/10.1007/978-3-030-55165-0_6

Victor Gorshkov is an associate professor at the Faculty of International Economic Studies, University of Niigata Prefecture (Japan). He previously served as a Dean at the Faculty of International Liberal Arts, Kaichi International University (Japan). He received his M.A. in international economics and finance from Khabarovsk State University of Economics and Law (Russia) and Ph.D. in Economics from Kyoto University (Japan). He is a charter member of the Japanese Society for Comparative Economic Studies. Victor has taught part-time at Kanagawa University, Rikkyo University, and Keio University in Japan and conducted research as a visiting scholar at the Institute of Economic Research, Kyoto University and the Slavic-Eurasian Research Center, Hokkaido University. His research interests are in the field of international economics, comparative economic systems, international business and emerging market economies. Victor's recent publications include the following: Gorshkov, V. (2024). Chapter 10. The Peculiar Features of Emerging and Transition Economies. pp. 196–210. In R. Wakasugi (ed.). *International and Regional Economy: Learning from the Foundations*. Tokyo: Bunshido (in Japanese); Gorshkov, V. (2022). Cashless Payment in Emerging Markets: The Case of Russia. *Asia and the Global Economy*, 2, 100033; and Gorshkov, V. (2020). Chapter 4. Fundamentals and Recent Trends in Russian Banking. pp. 73–93. In S. Rosefielde (ed.). *Putin's Russia: Economy, Defence and Foreign Policy*. Singapore: World Scientific Publishers.

SPRINGER NATURE

GPSR Compliance

The European Union's (EU) General Product Safety Regulation (GPSR) is a set of rules that requires consumer products to be safe and our obligations to ensure this.

If you have any concerns about our products, you can contact us on ProductSafety@springernature.com

In case Publisher is established outside the EU, the EU authorized representative is:

Springer Nature Customer Service Center GmbH
Europaplatz 3
69115 Heidelberg, Germany

The manufacturer's authorised representative in the EU is Springer Nature Customer Service Centre GmbH, Europaplatz 3, 69115 Heidelberg, Germany. If you have any concerns regarding our products, please contact ProductSafety@springernature.com

Printed and bound by CPI Group (UK) Ltd, Croydon, CR0 4YY

23/03/2026

02076360-0004